Beyond Coral Shores

Inggoy, the Batangan blacksmith
Hannah Chester Haworth

Beyond Coral Shores
Life and Work with a Remote Tribe

Martin C. Haworth

Authentic

First published 2006 byAuthentic Media
9 Holdom Avenue, Bletchley, Milton Keynes, Bucks, MK1 1QR, UK
285 Lynnwood Avenue, Tyrone, GA 30290, USA
OM Authentic Media
Medchal Road, Jeedimetla Village, Secunderabad 500 055, A.P.
www.authenticmedia.co.uk
Authentic Media is a division of Send the Light Ltd., a company
limited by guarantee (registered charity no. 270162)

British Library Cataloguing in Publication Data
A catalogue record for this book is available from the British Library

ISBN-13: 978-1-85078-665-8
ISBN-10: 1-85078-665-8

Cover design by fourninezero design.
Print Management by Adare Carwin
Printed in Great Britain by J.H. Haynes & Co., Sparkford

To the memory of my niece, Vicky Lewis (1979–1993)
whose sense of fun, in spite of long illness,
was an inspiration.

Contents

Acknowledgements

I wish to express a big thanks to Anne Cameron for her patient editing of this material and for her encouragement to pursue publication.

Introduction

Missionary biographies tend to be read by relatively few Christians and are mostly written with them in mind. *Beyond Coral Shores* strives toward a broader appeal, telling all that's humorous and insightful about adapting to a very basic life in a remote, tribal setting. As the spiritual emphasis is already stated in my book, *Smoking the Mango Trees* (Monarch Books), this story is hopefully accessible to those who wouldn't read a missionary biography. It aims to address the interests of those who remain curious about the lifestyle changes in the great traverse made when engaging in depth with a culture that is the antithesis of one's own background.

And yet this book is wholly relevant for those preparing to become missionaries and for those who follow them prayerfully on the homeside. It is an honest tale about being prepared by a God who calls, enabling those who are sent and those who receive, to genuinely love one another. Without love, any knowledge that we seek to pass on to benefit others in such a context, often fails. This is a timely reminder in an age where so much emphasis is put on professionalism, that any great learning in the fields of anthropology, theology and linguistics, will not enable us to truly engage at depth if we do not have real love for those we serve.

Missionaries are accused of harming cultures, of blundering in with their own agendas. Hopefully missions have largely learned from past mistakes. This is one account of coming to a people whose traditional values were already being challenged by an unsympathetic outside world. This is about our response to affirm a tribe in all that was wholesome about their culture and to help them overcome their fears and their doubts. It's about addressing basic needs: preventing unnecessary deaths, enhancing livelihoods and providing literacy skills, in a heartfelt endeavour to give dignity to a tribal people anxious to take their place in a wider world.

The Philippines – Mindoro Island
Copyright © OMF – www.omf.org.uk

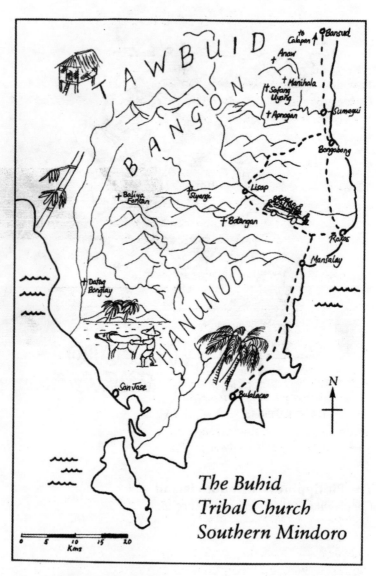

The map shows:

TAWBUID

BANGON

HANUNOO

to Calapan
Bansud
Anaw
+ Manihala
+ Safang Uyang
+ Apnagan
Sumagui
Bongabong
Lisap
Siyangi
+ Baliya Fontan
+ Batangan
Roxas
Mansalay
+ Datag Banglay
San Jose
Bulalacao

N

0 5 10 15 20
Kms

The Buhid
Tribal Church
Southern Mindoro

The Buhid Tribal Church
Martin Haworth

To the Ends of the Earth

Passing the tense melee of the four-forty fast trip,
Of the anxious, who in saving two hours lose the whole day,
We opt for the slow, the not so scheduled,
Rusty ferry that sails about sunset.

Casting off from the oily wharfs and stifling steel sheds,
The ferry crouches past huge liners out in the bay,
On a course set for the crimson sinking sun,
Ambling at a pace that can't be measured
Against the distant shore as shadows sprawl.

Out here – crossing slow leagues of sea –
The moment's ripe to just let go
Those chasings of the past mad days
And sink into the unhurried rhythm
Of the softly-singing engines.

Scorning time, a snatch of eternity's calm
Is ours all voyage long across the wide straits,
As the sunset fades on stirred waters.
Quite viscous now, the mercury sea
Is strangely charged an electric blue
Under the gathering embrace of a tropical night.

Candescent bursts from a hundred or so pressure lamps
Blossom in the velvet night all sea long
From as many outriggers previously unseen.
In their pond skater-like craft, the fishermen
Appear so frail and lonely on the ocean's immensity,
Like pilgrims plying some unseen trail
Beneath the silhouetted rim of the world's edge.

To the ends of the earth we have come,
To remote mountains and a roadless interior;
Our journey's end among a gentle tribe
Who received us as their own in what seems an age ago.

                                        Martin C. Haworth

Glossary of Terms

Mangyan: the collective name for the six tribes who inhabit Mindoro Island

Kano: abbreviated form of *Amerikano*, an appellation given to all white foreigners

Calapan: provincial capital of Oriental Mindoro, Mindoro Island

Mangyan Bible School: established by OMF for the training of leaders for the Mangyan Tribal Church

'Ductor: abbreviation of conductor, the bus fare collectors

Buhid: Mangyan tribe located in the southern part of Mindoro

NPA: New People's Army – a Marxist rebel group active in upland Mindoro and other parts of the Philippines

Chefoo: an OMF boarding school for primary age children

Luktanon: a Batangan Buhid term referring to all non-Mangyan Filipinos

Faduwasay: Buhid word for either brother or sister

Fotol: Buhid for machete

Tagalog: a considerable people-group – also refers to the language they speak

Aswangs: ferocious spirit beings said to be half-man, half-bird

Bangka: an outrigger canoe

Author's Note: Tagalog language has borrowed some Spanish words which are largely transliterated as they feel fit. I have reproduced Filipino spelling and their usage, correct or otherwise, as Filipino Tagalogs would use them. Accordingly, piso and not peso is the currency of the Philippines.

Chapter One:

Out of Sync

'Ahas – ahas!' screeched our househelp, backing away from me with a look of horror across her face. She had asked me to replace the heavy gas container from the corner of the kitchen that I was duly carrying to the back door. Being newly arrived in the Philippines I did not know what *ahas* meant and our househelp, forgetting we didn't yet understand much Tagalog, had blurted out with alarm what was clearly a warning.

Once she had regained some composure, she helpfully pointed at the base of the gas bottle that I still had in my hands. Looking in the direction indicated, the evident horror in her expression was immediately reflected in my own. Just at knee height where the base of the gas container reached, writhed a small black snake emerging from the recess of the container's hollow base where, in that quiet and dark corner of the kitchen, it had been discreetly slumbering.

So that's what *ahas* meant!

Part of the new programme being introduced in the language school we daily attended was being drilled through the 'direct approach'. This consisted of pointing at objects and speaking the Tagalog word for such, without the use of any other language, just in the same manner a child learns. I never had any problem remembering the word for snake after that. With the sound of our househelper's voice being forever associated with the word *ahas*, it became difficult to pronounce without imitating the same note of alarm.

1

Immediately placing the gas container on the floor before it struck my legs, I trapped the snake between floor and container rim. I looked for a piece of wood to kill the writhing snake. Not finding any such implement, I took hold of one of the heavy, wooden dining chairs and turning it upside down, stabbed at the snake's head with the back of the chair rest. As the chair's back was not of uniform level, I missed most of the time, making the snake angry and causing it to strike out. When I eventually dispatched it I had quite an audience, for during my lengthy battle, Rhodora – our househelp – had summoned help from the neighbouring terrace of apartments. One of these, a young lad turning twenty, asked if he could keep the dead snake as a souvenir. I was glad to hand it over, not knowing quite what to do with it.

A colleague in another city once had a cobra enter through her front door. She had run outside for help and there summoned two policemen who were nearby. Maybe this was the first occasion they had been called upon to legitimately use their firearms, and with it being in defence of a vulnerable female, a foreign woman at that, the situation appealed to their chivalrous instinct and occasioned a sportive display of their shooting skills. Most of the bullets hit the furniture and walls. The thought of ricocheting bullets probably being of greater danger than the snake itself did not seem to enter the thoughts of these zealous policemen. Eventually a lucky stray in this incessant stream of bullets hit the snake's head!

Alexandra – my wife – had not been around during this heroic battle with the back of a dining chair against a ferocious snake, protecting both the frightened Rhodora and Iain and Hannah, our two small children, from what I assumed was a deadly, venomous reptile. When

Alexandra came back from the language school later that morning, four of us regaled her with the incident. She disbelieved us at first until we insisted she take a look at the proof in our neighbour's house. When she saw the half-foot length of this thin specimen, placed in an empty fish tank, she laughed!

Did I detect a note of derision? Yes it was only small, but then so are many deadly things like Black Widow spiders and the tiny Egyptian asp that took Cleopatra's life! I did not know at the time that this 'House Snake' – or 'Sleeping Snake', as Filipinos refer to them – was quite harmless. Some Filipinos maintain they are venomous, probably owing to their not wanting to make any fatal mistakes.

Our family of four had arrived in the Philippines only a month earlier and we were still in those early stages of finding our feet in a new country with a new organisation. We had our struggles with a language that bore no resemblance to any European language with the exception of a generous sprinkling of Spanish words. But then the Spanish words had to be learned in addition to the Tagalog equivalents for they had not replaced the national vocabulary but rather enriched it with alternatives.

Our first impressions had not been too favourable, bearing out a Chinese businessman's commiseration with a group of us who had raised a hand in response to his asking his audience, which of us were bound for the Philippines? We were still back in Singapore at that time, the clean, orderly state where chewing gum was banned, as too was the carrying of the smelly fruit – durian – on the underground. Singapore was a model city, law-abiding, a jewel in the new emerging Asia, paragon of a tiger economy.

Manila had been a shock. We had arrived at an orderly international airport, which contradicted all the warnings we had received from those keen to steel us against the culture shock. Surely they had been joking at our expense or had grossly exaggerated the contrast between the super-efficient Singapore with this economic laggard. We emerged from the airport's air-conditioned precincts to be confronted by humid heat, choked with diesel fumes and a sort of cooking oil smell. A delirious sea of faces greeted us on crossing the road separating the arrival hall from the sprawl of a car park. Bodies several rows deep, pressed forward onto the crowd control barriers scanning the newly arrived for a familiar face, whilst security guards looked on, dubiously viewing the barriers. Relatives had come to meet their spouses or siblings returning from overseas contracts, many of whom were making their first trips home after two or three years abroad in places such as Saudi Arabia, Malaysia, Japan, Hong Kong and Singapore.

These welcome-home well-wishers were banned from the airport. Extended families arrived here en masse, hiring entire jeepneys and coming equipped with their pots of rice and whole pigs roasted on a spit to properly receive their beloved. Many had benefited from regular bank transfers and were keen to exhibit their indebtedness to honour their benefactors. At one time, apparently, the partying started within the airport precincts, making it impossibly congested as passengers and well-wishers picked their way through families dividing out generous portions of the glazed stuffed boar onto a spreading circle of plastic plates. These jubilant family groups had since been relegated to the car park, contained behind barriers and eyed by guards with machine guns.

In this sea of thousands of faces we were to pick out one face we had never seen before – the face of an

Irishman. Look as hard as we could, we didn't spot Mr Strachan but saw so many who obviously weren't male and Irish in this collage of Asian features. He found us, a tired, bewildered family accompanied by other equally bemused and wilting westerners, just resigned to the waiting game of hanging about until someone claimed us. Mr Strachan had come with a tiny sign with the initials 'OMF' – the name of our organisation – written in what looked like turquoise crayon. The sign had little to commend itself other than its handy size, easy to fold up neatly and stuff into the pocket when not in use. Judging by its near illegibility, it had been very handy now for several years!

We were shown to an old van, a chassis turned out from one of those Asian street-side welding shops, box shaped and rickety, with tiny perspex windows that let in too little of the stuffy, unsatisfying breeze. Mr Strachan had brought a Filipino driver who had the unenviable task of reversing out into a sea of people all ant-heap-busy. Riding the back step of the OMF van, the small Irishman shouted instructions through the open rear door to the driver, who dutifully edged backwards. These instructions were supplemented by an eclectic code consisting of various hand rhythms made on the roof of the van. A jeepney blasted its 80-decibel klaxon, dividing the human tide that miraculously came together again immediately on what should have been a clear stretch of street behind the departing jeepney.

Mr Strachan was in his mid- to late fifties, bald down the centre and grey around the sides. His hair, in stressed disarray, absorbed the alternating colours of the red, yellow and blue lights that adorned in impressive displays the front kanga bar of the passing jeepneys.

Somehow seven of us squeezed into the back of this incommodious van which already had looked full with our luggage before we clambered in. A child was on one lap, another sat on a suitcase. It was dark outside and all that could be seen for a long while were rows of headlights behind and partially illuminated vehicle interiors providing brief glimpses of smoking men dressed in under-vests. These were the drivers of the passenger jeepneys, holding wreaths of various bank notes secured between fingers, giving them the appearance of bookies. Were they taking bets on how many more they could possibly squeeze on board their overloaded jeepney? Perhaps they set the odds on how long it would take at this stop and crawl pace to reach the skyscraper business district of Makati, or the low rise sprawl of Bonnie Avenue and the busy markets and cheap shopping malls of Cubao. We edged forward, windows wide open, vainly attempting to reduce the sweat pouring off our brows and trickling down our backs. The noise of the traffic throbbed on all sides; clapped-out trucks and jeepneys, every third vehicle rattling away with what sounded like a specially fitted tin disk flap mounted on the exhaust manifold to accentuate the revving of the engine. When the engine revved, this disk purposely rattled with a reverberation that thrilled the Filipino male.

On one squalid street corner, a group of men, tanned more than the other Filipinos around them, wore little more than a G-string. These were of the Mangyan tribes, hired from the provinces of Mindoro Island for the seasonal work of daubing silver paint over dead tree saplings, sold as Christmas trees for silly prices! What would we have thought had we the foreknowledge that we would live among this tribal group.

Makati was passed with the high rise associated with a bustling capital city and once again the urban sprawl stretched about us as we laboriously progressed in and out of commercial districts, where retail and street-side manufacture combined. A glass-fronted showroom stood hemmed in by oily workshops of crumbling concrete and shanty shacks of old twisted corrugated iron and plywood, even cardboard, which in this impoverished country is sold flat-packed at the back of supermarkets for the cost of a bag of peanuts. Still the same traffic congestion kept us at best to a crawling pace, slower than the movement of busy people pressed along the pavements, weaving between street vendors selling wares laid out on the walkway. Children ran the gauntlet of the five-laned traffic, selling cigarettes and newspapers, others merely begging, knocking on the closed windows of the air-conditioned class who might spare some pisos.

Three hours later, still appearing to be in the thick of Manila, the van turned abruptly off the main road beside some workshops and waste strips of oily puddles and rank weeds. The van revved with bravado before charging up a long ramp-like drive towards a walled enclosure on top of a hillock. With a toot of the horn, high metal gates parted before us and we entered a different realm of orderliness, yet still concrete-grim, the world of the compound, shutting out another shanty behind its high walls. The organisational headquarters were modest, looking the poorer relation of the few private homes about. Private homes bore the same fortress-like appearance, deeply wary of the underworld of drug addicts, thieves, murderers and rapists and all other such miscreants needing to be shut out by broken glass-topped walls and coils of barbed wire.

We awoke the next morning still delicate from the grimness of those first impressions of that interminable journey made the night before from the airport, impressions made more poignant compared with the orderly and fascinating Singapore. Could it really have been so bad?

A small garden outside the dining room soothed my troubled nerves. Half of the garden was under the inviting shade of a bushy palm tree where hibiscus and creepers made a concerted effort to almost disguise the gruesome ten-foot walls barricading us in from the harshness of what lay beyond.

'Good morning, morning!' greeted Mr Strachan with the beaming smile and shiny complexion of a man now at peace with the world. I studied him carefully for a moment, incredulous that this was the same man who had anxiously directed our reversing van through the melee the night before. With a roguish twinkle in his eye, he went on to announce, 'Today you will have more or less free. Do a bit of shopping for the things you forgot to bring with you. Our driver will take you in the van to Cubao...' he added in a most matter-of-fact tone occasioning a Celtic twinkle, '...from where you will make your own way back!'

As co-ordinator for new and short-term workers, Mr Strachan always relished the mild shock guaranteed to register on the faces of a few nerve-frayed newcomers.

The nightmare impressions I had happily closed my weary eyes upon the night before, which I rationalised must have been all too exaggerated by having arrived tired in a strange city, now seemed a world away. Breakfasting on familiar food and at leisure beside the tranquillity of the palm-shaded garden helped restore my equanimity.

In a little while, we, Mr Strachan and some other newcomers boarded that square van of the night before, more accommodating now discharged of that mighty pile of luggage, and were duly led off to market. Passing through the ponderous metal portals crowned with spikes, the van descended the hillock with almost a sense of reluctance as the awful reality was enjoined. I had not over-exaggerated the squalor, or the total absence of the lovely. In fact, it was worse by day! The sun revealed the rubble and rubbish that darkness had managed to partly conceal, and exposed men urinating against the wayside walls and naughty children being severely reprimanded by life-is-hell mothers, spilling out from the shanties.

What on earth had induced us to give up our own thriving guest house business in the Highlands of Scotland to come to this? It was no romantic notion, for the reports and photos of others who had come from the Philippines had graphically portrayed the reality, but not so thoroughly as to prevent our being shocked now. We had been drawn here because of the needy and the poor whose spiritual hunger had been aroused by the absence of all the material props that the western world builds its security upon. We were there at the invitation of the Filipino Church.

A smiling Mr Strachan, relishing every moment of our discomfort and bemusement, deposited us at Cubao. Equipping us with the office telephone number, a just-in-case precaution, he pointed over to a section of road quite chock-a-block with buses and jeepneys vying for trade and remarked, 'There you will find a bus with the destination of "Fairview" that'll bring you back. Tell the conductor you are going to Diliman. Failing that, jump on board any jeepney with the same sign and ask to be put down near "Feria"!'

We didn't think to question the two different destination names for the same place of disembarkation. We were bewildered, but we made allowances for the fact that this was Manila – what seemed not to make sense in our home setting probably did here.

We took a turn of the wet market made brief by the fish stench and sight of laid out pigs' entrails. We found refuge in an air-conditioned electrical shop where we bought some torches and batteries involving the services of five Filipinas. One wrote the receipt, another took that to the cashier who in turn gave another the invoice to present back at the counter to claim the purchase. This was not ours until it was finally inspected at the door by a uniformed girl armed with a cane who briefly poked into the carrier bag in a show of inspection. What a job creation scheme! Now equipped for those unexpected power cuts we had been warned about that could last for hours, we made our way over to the buses and jeepneys.

Seeing a party of seven westerners aroused the excitement of a number of bus and jeepney conductors who shouted various destinations with earnestness that suggested we were in imminent danger unless we boarded their bus there and then. Some even took us by the arm in an attempt to bring us on board, taking us for the lost and bewildered foreigners we felt ourselves to be. Not all were so much intent on seeing us safely back to our desired destination but were more motivated by the thought of selling us seven tickets, no matter the direction, and preferably all the way to the depot. It was the Swiss couple in our party, Thomas and Brigitte, who, having been in Manila just a year before, were more alert to what was going on. They knew where to look to determine which was the destination plaque amidst the display of pictures and names plastered across the front windscreens.

Immediately above the jeepney windscreens, stretching the entire width of the vehicle, were chrome plaques depicting colourful and highly stylised calligraphy. On this, the owner would stamp something of his identity, a name of a sweetheart or a child, a place name like 'Saudi' showing an indebtedness to the country where he had made the money to buy the jeepney. Sometimes written there was a phrase, an aspiration, like 'King of the Road'. The fact that this huge chrome plaque was probably 50 times larger than the tiny plastic plaque suctioned onto the windscreen showing the jeepney's destination, indicated something of the Filipino's sense of priority; image being of greater importance than practicality.

When new, with whole panels of the shiniest chrome gleaming (and there was much chrome on a jeepney), jeepneys were indeed impressive to behold, with their superfluous six, eight, even ten long silver antennae bristling preposterously from the bonnet, of such length that sometimes they had to be arched over and secured to the roof. Twin chrome horse models occasionally adorned the bonnet, making a Mercedes symbol look particularly beggarly. Attached to the front bumper, or kanga bar, was an impressive arrangement of coloured headlights and fog lamps, not that there was ever any fog in the tropics down at sea level.

The driver's view through the windscreen narrowed by the application of mirror foil along the top and bottom of the windshield, obscured nearly all the view, leaving only an alarmingly thin strip of vision of the road ahead. Mounted on the dashboard were the ubiquitous images of either Mary or the Santo Nino, the child Jesus dressed up with all the royal pomp of one of the Stuart kings of Britain (or rather their Spanish counterparts of that era), with velvet cloak and gold brocade adornment and long hair curled into ringlets. The images were believed to give protection. Some drivers, sensitive to the association such images have to idolatry, had Bible texts instead written on laminated card stuck to the windscreen. The appearance of all these scriptural texts gave the impression of a people deeply rooted in the Bible. But these verses were generally more to serve the same purpose as the image – a talisman to give protection.

The jeepney's interior was often as impressive as its exterior, with its upholstered seats of red imitation leather dimpled with button studs, and sometimes the ceilings were adorned with mosaics of glass stretching the entire length, the effect finished off with the garish embellishment of coloured lights. Yes it was over the top, but it didn't pretend to be otherwise and was unashamedly boastful and brash, a celebration of popular art.

The most important accessory to all jeepneys was the sound system. Capable of pumping out an excessively high wattage, the music was still dominant even when driving pell-mell with the rush of wind through the long open panels that made up the side window apertures. Even when standing still with the noise of traffic, horns and street vendors all about you, the music still dominated, encapsulating the passengers in the glitzy otherworldliness, transporting one far from the grim realities round about.

We passed a phenomenal display of huge film poster hoardings we recollected seeing earlier and the palisade of the national mint, double fenced, surveyed by CCTV cameras and protected by perimeter microwave sensors. These two landmarks gave a reassuring familiarity that at least so far, we were heading along the right road.

I relaxed until a Filipino tapped me on my wrist. He dropped a pile of coins into my hand. Why was he giving me this money? Thomas reached for my hand and I dutifully released the money. He seemed to be expecting this payment and since I was not, I had no reason to hold on to it. Fares were collected by passengers passing money from one to another, the money all ending up at the front in a tray or recess made there on the dashboard. I have often wondered what the reaction would be, if playing the naïve foreigner, I thanked the one offering the fare before pocketing it?

For a long while, the scenery was all unremarkably the same and I began to wonder whether we were still on the right road. How were we to know where to get off? I had forgotten to take particular note of the surroundings that led to our fortress-like, office-cum-guest-home. I might as well have given in to that almost overwhelming desire to sleep which the rest of my family had succumbed to, for Thomas remained alert. The Swiss have a natural discipline drilled into them through their formative years, to take heed of all such practical details. True to his race, Thomas had duly noted the filling station shortly before and the immense illuminated Coca-Cola sign that rose immediately after the compound. He signalled the driver to stop at exactly the base of the long ramp that led to the fortress on the rise.

Chapter Two:

Dancing Between Clashing Bamboo

The unlovely clamour of Manila receded somewhat over the coming months for we were whisked away, after just three days in Manila, to study Tagalog language in an interminable fashion at the OMF language school in Batangas. Singles managed to get through the course in less than twelve months but we were way off target. But then we were also home schooling our three- and five-year-old children, as everyone reasoned in an attempt to pacify our distress.

Batangas is a port city, very much provincial and whilst still displaying the many disagreeable aspects of Manila, one could better cope since the squalor was on a smaller scale. For instance, the abject poverty of the squatter communities in every quarter with all the attendant crime induced by the desperation their circumstances imposed was just as evident here in Batangas as in Manila. We had our own apartment, close to the river forming the natural eastern boundary of the city. From the back bedroom window, looking out across the painted corrugated iron rooftops to the fields, palm trees and hills under a blue sky cast an alluring spell. Hannah wistfully referred to the countryside beyond the river as 'Fairyland', in contrast to the noise, fumes and squalor of the shanty round about us. The sight of distant Mount Halcon beckoned with its stimulating, wind-blown cape of cloud. Such a distant sight soothed the claustrophobic sensation felt by being pent up in the city. In the cool of the late afternoon, we often took the children down to the river bank, sat on top of the cracked concrete flood barrier, and watched the tropical sunset hues extinguish on the passing waters of the murky river. We lingered, savouring the dwindling moments until these expired with our momentary sense of euphoria. There we forgot the language blunders and cultural misunderstandings of the day, but the resilient foreboding that this was a language we were never going to master was not long in coming to the fore once again.

At first Tagalog had seemed easy. Written in Latin script and without the tones of many Asian languages, Tagalog appeared deceptively accessible. The scattering of some familiar-sounding Spanish words together with American English words, both spelt as Filipinos saw fit, further made Tagalog-learning look straightforward. We reckoned we would soon be conversing with ease with Filipinos. Alexandra had a French degree and was naturally gifted at languages, a fact compounded by close on a 100 per cent score which she gained in a language aptitude test we had both sat during the interview process with the organisation. I was not such a suitable candidate, only getting half my wife's score, but my spoken Arabic and Italian had been taken into account, languages I had partly acquired more through sheer diligence than from any natural flair.

Our days were structured solely around acquiring this oriental language. The school part of the formal language study programme consisted of two hours of language drills a day, a one-to-one study with a Filipina teacher. The school was not in an office-like building, but a villa converted by a carpenter who had erected tiny cubicles, with just enough room for two people to face one another over a desk. As the partitions of the cubicles were not from floor to ceiling and were accessed through a curtain rather than a door, one could hear fellow students making the same blunders, mispronouncing their drills and executing the same excruciating grammatical errors. This bosh made of the national language was met with patience from the female teachers and boredom from the two male teachers, one of whom fell asleep during one of my oral assignments.

However, my wife tells me that the male teachers were particularly attentive, making encouraging gestures by rapidly raising the eyebrows, or raising a single brow to stop the student at a fault. During this pause they would incline forward across the desk with open mouth, willing the right words from the hapless female's mouth.

Apart from preparing for these lessons and reviewing the material afterwards, which together with assignments formed the four-hour study time at home, the other main emphasis of the course encouraged us to get out into the marketplace and use what had been learnt. Shopping was soon mastered, an impressive vocabulary built up, but frustration was never far off when you aspired to greater heights than ordering a kilo of the sweeter mangoes. If we were to relate at the profounder level of people's thoughts and engage with their spiritual aspirations, all these fine bargaining phrases learned were not going to stand us in much stead! We could mimic beautifully phrased Tagalog, impressing Filipinos until they thoughtlessly replied, invariably not choosing the phrases set out in the textbook or discourteously slipping into the then unintelligible colloquial!

A fellow student who made regular sorties into the market lacked the ability to say no. Some of the items she purchased were required in her household, but more often than not, she came home with mops and brushes, or bagfuls of strange-looking vegetables she had no idea how to prepare. Should they be eaten at all or used to dye one's hair? She had more glassware than there was room for in her substantial cabinet. One could picture the market vendors greeting her gleefully, alerting all the neighbouring sellers of the arrival of this likeable and gullible foreigner, exceptional for her insatiable need of whatever they sold.

Although such sorties were not helpful to her bank balance, these encounters were as much a therapy as a language opportunity. She would be hailed with a barrage of greetings, doing wonders for her self-esteem (which all students found floundering much of the time), and as time passed, she became more knowledgeable about their families and they of hers, developing more meaningful relationships. Having all come out from some useful employment or other back home, we new arrivals, committed to operating in the local language, soon discovered we had little to contribute to the general welfare, other than the tiresome expectation of dispensing the hoards of money that all white foreigners have an inexhaustible supply of.

After several months of being cooped up in the city, we were encouraged to get a driving licence and borrow the organisation's van to visit some of the natural wonders about us. I presented myself at the traffic division of the police station, filled in the required forms and duly presented these to be checked over and stamped at various counters. After a couple of hours being sent from desk to desk, waiting my turn in the substantial queues, I received a form to take to a certain optician down the street for an eye test.

The optician had his practice up on the second floor. Mounting the stairs to that level, the reception desk confronted me. The desk occupied the small landing in front of a door leading into a suite of rooms. I presented my form to the white-uniformed receptionist, made the required payment and then was asked, 'Do you wear glasses?' When I replied that I didn't, she wrote the conclusion on the form, '20:20 vision'! She rubber-stamped the form before returning it.

'So what do I have to do now?' I naively asked since I was neither instructed through to the office nor told to wait. The receptionist looked up from her desk surprised at this curious question. 'That's it. You go back to the police station now to show them that you have passed the eye test!'

After jumping through a few more hoops at appropriate desks and counters, I was informed that my licence would be ready in two to three months' time! Noticing my crestfallen expression, the clerk explained that I could drive on the strength of the small square invoice with which I had been issued.

Just a few days later, encouraged by the comparative ease with which I had secured my driving licence, an Irish colleague decided to apply. She had to go to all the same desks and the optician, but in addition, had been made to sit a theory test. Moreover, much to her chagrin, she failed in spite of having passed her British driving test just a year or two before.

'Well, what am I supposed to do now?' she complained to the clerk in a stroppy, no-nonsense tone of voice.

'Let me have a look,' requested the clerk. He ran his eyes over the test paper, then over this attractive Irish girl, nodded knowingly and came round the other side of the counter with a conspiratorial air and a new form in his hand.

'Here – do it again,' he said, placing another test paper down. 'And I think you may need this too,' he added, placing a printed form beside the test paper. She was about to protest, commenting that it was going to make little difference, when she noticed that the latter form placed by her question paper was none other than the answer sheet! She did not allow the irregularity to bother her since she regarded the whole thing a farce anyway, being failed when she was quite competent to drive.

The clerk wandered over a few minutes later, and noting she was almost onto the final page, took up the answer sheet, saying, 'We can't have you getting them all correct can we? Someone might think you have cheated!' He put the answer sheet away in his desk and whilst waiting for her to finish, ripped up her first test paper into increasingly smaller pieces.

A few months later, I helped a Welsh girl through this process. This time, there was no test. But her undoing had been the dual language layout on this Welsh version of the UK driving licence.

'How do we know that the English on this licence is a true translation of your language?' the clerk asked in that deliberately awkward manner of one angling for a bribe. He would not listen to reason and eventually tossed the wad of application papers across the desk. 'Go to the British embassy and obtain a letter from them, testifying that the English is a true translation of your language.'

'But the embassy is in Manila!' remarked the Welsh girl and elaborated at length with her quaint accent and a very conversational manner in her defence. I don't know whether it was anything she said, or that her pretty appearance worked a change of heart in the stubborn heart of this official, but he picked up the papers, rubber-stamped them and issued her with the paper for the optician. Half a day later, when she received her small square certificate enabling her to officially drive before the licence proper was issued, she noticed the statement 'Greek' had been typed in as her nationality! She was all for having it rectified.

'Whilst you are driving a vehicle in the Philippines,' I said under my breath, 'you are Greek! All right?' I whisked her away before further complications arose and we trespassed too far on the patience of bureaucratic officialdom.

Equipped with driving licences we took the vehicle appropriately nicknamed 'Rattles' and, filling it full with fellow students and picnics, set off for the coast. Taal Volcano was a most memorable outing. Formerly the volcano had been massive and, having erupted violently on several occasions with devastating effect on the neighbouring towns and villages, had evolved into something totally different. The former volcano, still evident by a huge circumference of hills, made up the outer perimeter ring of probably more than twelve miles in circumference. Within this enormous ring lay a substantial lake. At one time this lake, which had been joined to the sea, became landlocked after an eruption. Today the freshwater lake infamously boasts of having the highest density of sea snakes found anywhere on earth! In the middle of the lake rises a sizeable volcanic island still very much active, with two cones, the higher of the two having its own crater lake within its rim. Thus Taal Volcano is two volcanic cones within a vastly greater volcanic crater, and a crater lake within a much larger one.

Making a flying visit to Asia, Alexandra's father was coerced across to the volcanic island. Being very fair complexioned (it was said of him that he got 'moonburn' on his holidays to the Costa Brava, turning red even though he only came out at night), he gamely assented to the hiring of mules to make the climb up to the crater rim. At midday we started our ascent up the treeless, steep hill, and were reminded of the ditty 'Only mad dogs and Englishmen go out in the midday sun'. We certainly had the place to ourselves. En route, my father-in-law exclaimed, 'This is quite ridiculous!', his puce features vividly set off against the white of his floppy sun hat. He turned back, vaguely fuming like the many rock fissures on the hillside issuing small spouts of steam, and set off back down the hill, leaving us to go on to the rim. There at the top, looking down the precipitous drop into the steamy crater, my wife sat down on a box-like structure. Only afterwards did we notice the writing on the side of this conveniently positioned seat. It stated that it was government property containing seismic measuring instruments. The next day we sheepishly read in the national newspaper that increased activity had been measured at Taal Volcano, and the surrounding communities were put on an alert footing to evacuate the area should the seismic activity increase further! Was this just coincidence or had this alarm been caused by my weary wife heavily sitting down on the instrument measuring box?

'Well, there was nowhere else to sit,' defended Alexandra, who somehow expected there to be a row of benches and picnic tables erected on this desolate, volatile rim of one of the frailest parts of the earth's crust on the brink of a regularly active volcano.

Rattles took us to the base of the hills surrounding Batangas. One day the children and I set off with Jay, an American colleague. Both our wives opting to stay at home left us in the unforeseen circumstances of being accompanied by two female students, the only other ones who had signed up for a full day's hike in the hills. As we commenced our climb up the mountain track, we stopped to admire a beautifully cultivated garden and Jay, having better Tagalog (being married to a Filipina), complimented the homeowner tending to his antirrhinums. Despite vocal protests from Jay, the owner picked a fair bunch of flowers and presented these to Jay.

'I should have known better than to have come out with those compliments!' remarked Jay, awkwardly clutching this bouquet of flowers as we moved on up the hill at the start of a serious mountain hike. As we laughed and chided Jay over his indiscretion, the delicate flowers wilted and became more and more battered despite the care Jay took. Eventually forced to give up on these flopped and now almost headless stems, he surreptitiously concealed these with a mixture of lament and relief inside a bush a few miles and a couple of thousand feet further on from the less-blooming garden.

A number of local farmers hailed us on our way and those we passed close to engaged us in conversation, wanting to know where we were going, whose were the two children and which of the two women was their mother? It reached the point when we cringed on encountering another person, enduring either the judgemental or roguish looks of the locals on learning that we had left our wives back at home and we were just off for the day with these two young girls. And we were missionaries too!

These trips brought great relief from a very pedestrian period of going through the frustrating routines of language learning, and observing church life but still not able to participate very meaningfully. Our teachers laid on cultural presentations and discussions when, putting aside their polite Asian reserve, they underlined all the cultural do's and don'ts to help us blundering foreigners more effectively blend into the local way of life and understand the Filipino mindset. They could be cruelly candid during these times, talking about 'amoy Kano' – the smell of an American (*Kano* being an abbreviated form of *Amerikano* that all westerners are deemed to be;

European countries are considered by many as just names of American states). Some reckoned this smell was due to the westerner's penchant for dairy products.

Unfortunately, I leaked copious amounts of sweat, which no amount of *tawas* (the local antiperspirant powder) and various antiperspirants could possibly stem the flow of. Filipinos had been taught through three centuries of Spanish colonialisation that it is highly improper to sweat, or at least to show any excess above the considered norm – a kind of faint sheen was the tolerated level. Sweating was the mark of a peasant, just as dirty fingernails are. Once this fact had been drawn to our attention, coupled with the over-zealous lady in a church we attended who would make a showy point of patting Alexandra's blouse to her sweaty back, we went around in a general state of mortification. I perspired all the more out of sheer embarrassment at my total inability to sweat less.

Part of this cultural reorientation was how to greet appropriately, which was often non-verbal. The mere raising of the chin or the eyebrows conveys a friendly hello, a confusing greeting at first when coming from the opposite sex, with its western connotations of flirting.

Our teachers put on delightful dance shows celebrating all that was flamboyant and graceful about Filipino culture. The school fraternity sought any excuse to stage such an event, like marking a *despedida* – the farewell party – of a student or member of staff from the language school. As *despedidas* occurred frequently in a school that had no set intake times, no month ever passed without the excuse to throw such a party. Two dances were guaranteed to be performed: the Spanish 'Fandango' more familiar to westerners than the lesser known 'Tinikling' of the Pacific.

For the Fandango, the female staff wore long Spanish costume dresses, elegant in their brightly dyed silk and chiffon with short puffed sleeves raised in elaborate crests above the shoulders. Before their entry into the room, the lights were extinguished and the crackly recording from an ancient gramophone record blurted out one of the many exuberant Iberian tunes, quite distorted as though this were a required part to enhance both the setting and the act. The dancers emerged with small red tumbler-like glasses filled with wax, burning in the gloom with magical quality, one in either hand and a third balanced upon the head. They went through a quaint routine of elegantly moving these fiery tumblers with all their flamboyant and natural oriental subtlety and grace, producing an enchanting effect.

The Tinikling required audience participation, calculated to fool the unsuspecting newcomer to the language school community. First a couple did a very straightforward display of this dance, daintily stepping in and out of two clashing bamboo poles. The rhythm was easy and predictable, produced not only by the two poles meeting together horizontally just above ground level but also by their being vertically struck downwards with a double beat onto a short bamboo section placed on the ground at right angles. All you needed were your wits about you to avoid a foot being trapped between the clashing poles. Your Filipino partner held your hand to guide and prompt you when to step and where to place your bared foot. You had to be totally uncoordinated to come a cropper at this initial stage.

No sooner had you the hang of the routine when the music would perceptibly increase in tempo and those bamboo poles clashed together with increasing alacrity. Then the feet had to begin to dance as never before with skill and great swiftness. The novice dancer's lower lip could be seen to be bitten more fervently and sweat beaded the brow (or in my appalling case would be already running into my eyes). Sooner or later, the inevitable occurred, a trapped foot of no hurt to limb, only damage to your pride.

Dancing the Tinikling with a Filipino dancer was something akin to learning a new language and culture. The first words and phrases came easily and the foreign ways held much initial charm; the experience was not just manageable but pleasurable, happily moving in one accord with your Filipino host. But the few phrases and scant cultural knowledge were not going to stand you in good stead for long. Furthermore, relationships carried a growing expectation of being able to converse more widely as well as increasingly more intelligibly! When the tempo picked up, the driving concern took over of striving to continue for as long as possible before being caught between the clashing bamboo. This was accompanied by a heightened awareness of no longer being entirely in sync with your Filipino partner, and in spite of every noble intention to the contrary, the dawning truth came of your being responsible for affecting the harmony of the movement. It became only a question of 'when', not 'if', your foot was going to be trapped!

After lengthy, formal speeches from everyone present, right down to the maintenance man, addressed to the graduated student, the mood was livened up again. Filipinos love playing party games – nothing too intellectual though, or demure, but of the more mindless variety; the more childish the better. Several of these games were variations of one and the same. Many of these had everyone seated in a circle when various people would rise at a certain password, there being several passwords pertaining to different players. This entailed moving onto the chair to your right, irrespective of whether someone was sitting there already. Of course once you had someone sitting on your lap, you couldn't move when your password was called and for the remainder of the interminable game you could well be pinned to the chair with five, six, even seven people sitting on top of you.

Who thought these games up? Foreign imports I suspect introduced to the parties of *Amerikano* children, games that Filipinos high-jacked. At Hannah's fourth birthday party we had invited a few Filipino children to our house. Understandably, being young and our being foreigners, their parents preferred to stay to look on. I had made a bilingual treasure hunt around the house which the children never really were given a chance to follow. From the start, the adults tore up and down the stairs, giggling and screaming, tugging at one another's clothes. They even pocketed the clues to scupper the chances of the opposition in full knowledge of contravening the instructions clearly stated before the beginning of the game. So disenchanted by the party, our two children could only be appeased by having a re-run once all the Filipinos had gone home! The onlooking Filipino children did not appear annoyed by their mothers, assuming the games were for the benefit of their parents. Their turn to enjoy themselves would come one day when they would become parents!

Once into our second year at the language school, we began to put into practice the very things we had come to the Philippines to do. Leading a Bible study with the househelpers and school cleaners was a requirement of the language course prior to graduation. Subjected to our still very inadequate skills, their oriental graciousness presented a polite countenance through our blundering attempts to edify. Alexandra took a study about eternal life and because the word for life –

buhay is close to the word for house – *bahay*, she spent the whole study talking about 'eternal housing', a very desirable and topical subject in a country afflicted by typhoons that devastated the shanty huts of the poor! Not one of them corrected her, not wanting Alexandra to lose face! Imagine the reactions an Asian might have if he or she were to lead an equally appalling study in a British language school to an audience of cleaners and a janitor!

Many are the blunders of those eager to be integrated, such as the young male missionary learning a tribal language. Whilst admiring a litter of puppies in a home he was visiting and wanting to express his appreciation, he turned to the young mother with a child at her breast and came out with the phrase: 'What beautiful breasts you have!' In that tribal language the word for puppy, apparently, was almost identical in sound to 'breast'. The young mum, who up to that moment had been unselfconscious about breastfeeding before him, quickly pulled her blouse together and retired into a back room of the house, no doubt wondering what kind of missionary had come to her village.

As part of a comprehension exam, we attended church with the school director and afterwards had to give a résumé of all that had been shared. One of the items in the three-hour long church service was a testimony from a woman who spoke ever so quickly in a very dramatic way, alternating from being sad and agitated one moment to being jubilant the next, really taxing our ability to follow. We had understood her to be talking about how she had been successfully treated for a vaginal cyst! She even produced an ultrasound photograph of this cyst and slowly rotated it before an impassive congregation. Surely we had not understood correctly! Not able to stand the suspense further, I leaned over to the school director and asked, 'Is she really talking about what I think she is talking about?' The director's equally incredulous expression confirmed that our comprehension skills were sharp.

Chapter Three:

To Misty Heights

Stationed at the ship's railing, a vantage point higher than the level of the rusty rooftops of the port's shanty, one could see only the taller buildings of Batangas city, emerging from what appeared to be an endless forest of coconut palms stretching into the distance. Out of this plain, Cuenca Mountain loomed remote, rising almost perpendicular with menacing volcanic aspect into the distant blue haze. The steep sides levelled to form a lip on either flank before the summit made a final rise forming an almost regular dome. Its remoteness lent it the appearance of being a painted backdrop, a giant petrified into rock standing sentinel to the approach of all seafarers. Behind this imposing mountain lay Taal Lake, out of which rose the active volcano, still rumbling and frequently breathing fire.

Looking seaward out into Batangas Bay and beyond to the Straits of Mindoro, the far more distant form of Mount Halcon beckoned across the South China Seas to the island of Mindoro. But for its great height and closeness to shore, it would not be seen from so far away. For months we had noticed it from the back of our flat beside the river, the bold sweep of its summit tantalisingly mingling with the clouds.

The crossing over to Mindoro was a memorable experience and one which subsequently rarely failed to refresh.

In the early 1990s, before the super-fast catamarans, the trip to cross the straits from the main island of Luzon to Mindoro took upward of three hours. The old, rusty ferryboats that still run the straits to this day with cargo and vehicles provided the only transport. It is this type of dilapidated ferry, notorious for being overloaded and ill-maintained, which combined with human error and adverse weather condition, accounts for the terrible loss of life and makes the international headlines. It was an unforgettable experience, boarding one of these floating coffins by the car deck. The narrow and steep, oily stairways smelling of diesel and urine in the sweltering heat, became treacherous in the crush of the impatient, pushing from behind. All three decks were full, hence the corridor commotion. Once the ship's engines started up, the metal panels working loose from their rusty rivets rattled alarmingly. Even before setting out onto the high seas, such an enormous volume of water flowed from the bilge pumps that one imagined water to be entering through the multitude of fissures as quickly as it was being pumped out.

A number of boys and a few older men in the water, shouting 'Piso' attracted the attention of those leaning over the ship's railings. Someone obliged, tossing a silver coin worth tuppence for them to dive for. When the piso-divers noticed our white faces, they frantically waved an arm, crying out, 'Hey Joe – Piso! Piso! Piso!'

'Hey Joe' is a Tagalog greeting to anyone who is white. Derived from formerly greeting US soldiers known as 'GI Joes' in this manner, any white person is similarly hailed.

Easier ways of making a living soon became more evident. Vendors wandered the decks selling individual cigarettes obligingly lit for their customers, boys brandished an impressive choice of newspapers and magazines, whilst more sold all manner of snacks from fried pig's intestine, semi-gestated hen's eggs, tangerines full of pith and pip, to peanuts. The wares were displayed in compartments and shelves on top ingeniously designed wooden trays slung from the vendor's neck. (When equipped with hooks and string, these trays suspended bags of crisps, wafers, sweets, bags of three boiled eggs complete with a pouch of salt, a clutch of quails' eggs and the small delicate pastries known as *opia* filled with a sweetened coconut. One had to admire the Filipino trader's imagination, whose enterprise dispensed with the traveller's need to journey with packed meals.)

I always thought there was only one way to eat peanuts: baked. But as this is a peanut-growing and peanut-loving nation, they were sold boiled in their shells, soggy and still warm, or shelled, fried in garlic and placed in the most slender paper or polythene bag. The more exotic peanut products were the peanut brittle, cakes of different circumferences held together by caramelised sugar, topped with sesame seed, and the thick wafer cakes of peanuts ground to a dust, mixed with sugar and lightly baked.

Dubious characters wandered the decks with their sing-song drawl of 'Manicure!' On second glance not all were the women you first took them for. These were the *bakla*, a Tagalog word our children picked up within their first 50 words, meaning 'transvestite'.

Gospel vendors set up their sound system on the middle deck so as to be heard by those on the decks above and below. (Those on a low budget bellowed through a megaphone.) After the memorised sermon, a bag was passed around as a 'love offering'. Such a gospel vendor boarded a public jeepney in Manila on which Alexandra was riding, that time thankfully not equipped with amplification. Having run through his usual spiel, the bag was passed round. Newly arrived in the country, my wife was both confused and afraid having understood nothing of the message and had mistaken the fanatic for a zealous terrorist exhorting money for 'the cause'.

What I found most offensive, more than exhorting folk to pay for a message of reconciliation that is God's free gift, was the detached tone of the preacher who showed no identification with his captive audience. He churned out his rehearsed lines like a salesman, appearing to have lost faith in his product. Never was an invitation made to respond (except by the giving of money) or an opportunity given for any troubled person to seek help.

With the preaching over and the vendors' ardour for plying their trade cooling after the initial flurry, people began to settle down into the rhythm of the voyage. Our eyes feasted on the extravagant natural beauty, as the ship pulled out of the deep indentation in the coast that is Batangas Bay and steamed onto the South China Seas proper. On a bearing south-west heading towards Calapan, we never moved far from the Luzon coast, until making for a large island rising alluringly verdant out of the dazzling blue sea. Further beyond, the hazy form of Mount Halcon beckoned the traveller to the promise of a romantic destination.

It was mid-September 1993 when Alexandra and I, with Iain and Hannah, sailed for Mindoro Island on a field trip from Batangas. Not knowing what a field trip would entail other than a ten-day relief from language drills, we anticipated adventure, and had a sense of determining what we might eventually be doing once we had mastered the language. To get out at last into the real Filipino world, away from the other blundering foreigners and ever-so-sympathetic Filipina language teachers was going to be a breath of fresh air. This field trip was to hopefully determine the type of work we could do and its possible setting.

Mount Halcon grew enormous on the approaching horizon as the ferry passed between two exquisite islands, pleasantly hillocked and bristling with palm trees. The island twins were large enough to provide a paradise for a rich recluse, giving the traveller a first glimpse of the magical tropics that they might wistfully had thought Manila would reveal. For one bare minute, the white coral shores fringed with coconut palms could be greedily admired. All too quickly, the ferry moved across the sun-kissed seas in the final half-hour journey to Calapan pier.

A low cliff rose beyond the pier, topped with palms caught in the sea breeze in an ecstasy of motion; inspirational, by my reckoning, to many an oriental folk dance. The heavy sea swell made it problematic for the pilot to dock, providing ample time to take in the new surroundings. Calapan looked poor, but we had not expected it to be otherwise. One- to two-storey houses, cheek by jowl, were tucked in the narrow strip between the rubbish-lined shore and the low, undulating hills capped with coconut, mango and bamboo groves. The silver dome of the Spanish cathedral reared a good way above the rust-red rooftops, which together with the twin spires of the Iglesia ni Cristo, dominated the skyline. Both were dwarfed by the grandeur of Mount Halcon emerging abruptly, no longer very distant, where summit and mist became indistinguishable at a considerable height, suffused in a radiance of tropical sunshine and humid vapour.

On entering the frenzied fray of the port, porters physically tried to relieve us of our travel bags and zealous conductors implored us to board their long-distance bus, deaf to our twice-repeated insistence that we were just staying in Calapan. The OMF mission home was both office and team base, with rooms for missionaries on the move or for those in need of convalescence. Set a short way up a hill, bounded by a superb garden of hibiscus and frangipani, the commotion of the port from this distance was no longer obvious and seemed caught in suspension, rather like a painting. The ferries came and went with a serene air. From this colourful garden, reality receded, a refuge from all that was cramped and sordid. Only the incessant drone of the 'traysikels' contending with the throaty rattle of the jeepneys racing one another along the long straight to the pier, kept one from letting go completely.

Calapan Pier
John Richards

Our field trip was not that busy, affording worthwhile time to reflect on our forward direction. Most of our companions at language school had a specific idea of what they had come to do, or knew the team they were welcome to join. We had no such comfort and seriously wondered why we had come to a land which already had growing churches that shared their faith with cheerful zeal to an undoubtedly needy world. How could we improve upon that with our fumbling Tagalog and our not-so-smiley faces? We were not seeking to do something better than the nationals but to fulfil a need not being met, to contribute something of lasting worth, to engage at depth and touch people's lives.

At the foot of mighty Halcon we passed the highlight of our field trip, in a more-civilised-than-expected bamboo house with broad polished floorboards of mahogany functioning as the self-catering guest house at the Mangyan Bible School. This centre, established by the mission to train future leaders of the Mangyan tribal churches, was staffed by Mangyan with the exception of one expatriate worker assisting in the upgrading of course materials.

Mangyan is the collective name for the six indigenous tribes who inhabit the mountainous interior of the island. In spite of being centuries-long neighbours, each tribe has its own language, and their cultures are often distinct from one another. Fear and suspicion had kept them separate, for in reality they were united only in family groups, uprooting home whenever someone died, driven by fear of the spirit of the dead. Their hunter/forest gatherer lifestyle kept them destitute and under-nourished in physical appearance and their isolationist preference made them exceptionally timid by nature. Like birds preferring to bide close to their nests hidden deep in the mountainous jungle, they rarely ventured beyond their mountain fastness until recently. Mangyan on the fringes had been pushed back into the hills by fellow Filipinos hungry for land – opportunists, landless and impoverished peasants from other islands, fugitives outlawed for crimes committed – all these flocked here, attracted by reports of free land.

Being non-confrontational, the Mangyan retreated from the threatening and sometimes violent encounters with these outsiders. Much maligned and despised, the Mangyan had been overlooked, no one wanting to champion their cause except for the missionaries who saw them as fellow humans, deserving of respect. The mission's work had first started here in the early 1950s, a whole generation of workers had come after the exodus from Communist-run China, and now the pioneers had almost all gone into retirement.

After overcoming their initial shyness, many Mangyan treated us as equals, not ingratiating themselves in the manner some do who have lived under the shadow of colonialism, envying our supposed great wealth. They did not behave in a jaunty, cool American manner, greeting us at every conceivable opportunity with 'Hey Joe', nor did they wrongly consider our ways probably better than their own. They had the ability to put their visitors at ease as they related to us as fellow humans whose behaviour and appearance intrigued and amused them.

Spared from the 333 years in a Spanish convent, which is how some refer to the period of Spanish colonialisation, the Mangyan were not perturbed by our sweating, for they freely perspired themselves without embarrassment. Similarly they had not been affected by the 48 years in Hollywood (equated with the term of American rule), and were not so aware of, nor lured by, the dazzle of riches. The drive for progress often breeds a discontent and inferiority amongst the minions craving to break out from their penury. The Mangyan though had developed in such isolation that apparently, three decades after the Second World War, a Japanese soldier living among them surrendered on just learning that hostilities had long since ceased.

Alexandra had the concern about what, if anything, we might have in common with tribal folk. How were we to be of any practical or spiritual help to such people? But as the days passed relating with the Mangyan at the school, Alexandra recognised that they were little different from ourselves behind the cultural trappings, having similar needs and concerns. We felt a strange affinity with these marginalised people and just wondered what needs there could still be that we might possibly meet.

Coming to this spacious guest home with running water and periodic electricity, we realised this was far from typical. If we were to work among the tribes, I wanted Alexandra to see what a truly authentic tribal village was like and the very basic conditions to which we would have to commit ourselves. Since I had had the opportunity to see such a village at Ayan Bekeg, I asked the principal to see if a day trip could be arranged.

A student from the college agreed to take us to Ayan Bekeg, a two- to three-hour climb up the mountain. Together with Helen – the eldest daughter of the school's principal – we set off before dawn. We had not slept particularly well in anticipation of this early start and had breakfasted without appetite on stale bread rolls and jam in the gloom of a guttering oil lamp. We traipsed along the path down the hill from the school to the village below, and beyond to the bridge crossing the mountain torrent, walking mechanically like sleepwalkers. The bridge was the worse for wear, with missing planks, swinging drunkenly as our small party crossed. A cold mist rising off the white waters brought us more to our senses.

West of the river the true climbing began, up along a deeply rutted logger's trail, winding relentlessly upwards, switching back through the steep jungle. Soon the dense forest swallowed up the distant roar of the river in the gorge below. Dawn had not yet broken and had this not been the tropics, no doubt there would have been a stillness in the air, a deep peace. But not so here. A multitude of insects and cicadas kept up their ceaseless buzzing and loud sawing noises, making the atmosphere feel charged with electricity. Even though the first light had not yet paled the eastern sky, the climb soon made us warm, so that I, at least, was already spotting the dust with the huge drops falling from my brow. Just as well we did not have to contend with the heat of the sunshine and had opted to set off at this unearthly hour instead.

Then the sun, as though in a hurry, unceremoniously rose.

We paused for a rest, looking down on the rice plains below, each paddy field swamped with water as though a river had burst its banks. Here and there, a row or grove of coconut palms stood out in silhouette against the gleaming sheets of water. On we trekked in the intensifying light, the children still eager to do it on their own. Laboured breathing left us speechless.

We stopped yet again, this time resting in a clearing where perched precipitously, we peered down on a minuscule world of paddy fields stretching like a huge patchwork quilt. Above, on Halcon's distant peak, white cloud periodically broke away from its parent streamer, sailing off in voluminous fragments, beautiful upon the tropic blue, mirrored in the extensive paddy flood. All day long we could have stopped just there, content to observe the changing scene. A river broke the uniformity of the plain, and an occasional road, unsighted until clouds of powder-like dust rose behind a speeding jeepney, interrupted the paddy field symmetry. Far below us now in the deep, tangled ravine, a flash of river could be glimpsed, its cascade inaudible at this altitude.

Hannah was later carried, perched on the broad shoulder of our guide. She sat there regally, not caring to look back at us, but always ahead, eager to view what the next turn in the trail would unfold. Another rest came, this time to draw water from a split bamboo laid in lengths like a conduit, supported by forked sticks pillared in the ground below its course, all the way from the unseen spring. The blood pounded in our heads as we searched for that invisible line where sky imperceptibly merges with sea.

After many more giddy halts on Halcon's side, and with the sun now nearing its zenith, Ayan Bekeg was reached – a scattering of bamboo huts raised on stilts, quiet and detached under the cogon grass thatch. Children ran indoors at our ungainly approach. We squatted in the shade, waiting for something to happen, taking our cue from Hermino who, now more than guide, had become our friend. Eventually a shy elder met us, scratching his head, his strong smile stained a betel-nut red. He beckoned us into a one-roomed hut, out of the dizzy glare of the sun where we gladly rose onto the bamboo floor platform and eased our sweat-saturated bodies onto the satisfying yield of split bamboo. There we lay awhile, our hearts palpitating far less and the sense of nausea and faintness passing. The waft of draught up through the slats was relished, as we gratefully ate that morning's baked *kamote* – the staple sweet potato – now cold in their jackets, grubby from the fire's ash.

The elder, remembering me from my previous visit made a few months earlier, complimented me on understanding far more now of what he was saying than before when I had unintelligibly grinned at him much of the time. He related the cares of his situation, providing valuable insight into the precarious position of an average tribal church. Not all was well and many were showing a change of heart, bored by what had become a tedious tradition. Ceasing to be relevant, many were no longer bothering to come to church. The boredom of being stuck in a rut with no expectation sounded all too familiar of many churches back home. But this elderly leader knew worship services when people praised God from their hearts, and listened avidly to sermons, and prayed in earnest. But he did not know how to restore what had been lost. Touched to be taken into his confidence, our prayer time together gave the elder that relief of having a burden shared.

I recalled my first visit and the small shack of a church filled with people, and the worship songs sung with a certain gusto which maybe our visit had occasioned. We had returned smiles shyly shot across the chapel, surprised by the simplicity of an earthen floor and the pulpit end of the church raised higher than the rest by merely terracing it out of the hillside. We left in a hubbub of farewells and flashes of smiles as the afternoon shadows lengthened, receiving a gift of food wrapped in banana leaf, thrust into a hand by children just overcoming their shyness.

Then, as now, we prepared to leave with growing reluctance for the plains, yet emotionally leaving far too soon, in everyone's estimation. One in spirit with these uncomplicated tribal folk, we the strangers, who had ventured out from beyond great oceans, from origins as diverse as their own, made our farewell, leaving their simplicity that so challenged our relative affluence. It was not only the length of the descent that made us linger at the last house, but real regret too at not having the time to get to know them better and enter more into their circumstances. They gathered on the edge of their village where we glanced back several times before the cloud separated us in that ethereal manner of mist.

Chapter Four:

A Trip to the Interior

Our family of four set off from Calapan at 5.30 a.m. in a rickety bus that drove along the potholed road at breakneck speed. The driver, being of the opinion that the brake was only for emergencies and for dropping off passengers, used the horn to devastating effect to clear pedestrians and slower traffic out of the way. Even the putting down of some passengers was executed swiftly, slowing only to a pace at which a person could leap off the running board and still hope to maintain their balance. The departing passenger would then do the final braking themselves by skilfully alighting on the side of the road, shod usually in flip-flops, whilst the bus sped on its way leaving a choking cloud of dust and diesel fumes.

After the field trip, we had returned to the routine of language school again, but now with a difference. We had a defined goal to aim for, a down-to-earth people to relate to, removing those nine months of doubt, wondering why we were in the Philippines. It took us another nine months though to complete the school course. During that time, Bob and Joy Hanselman, retired workers with the Buhid Mangyan tribe located in the southern part of Mindoro, came to check some translation they had been working on during their retirement in the States. They invited us to come and spend a weekend with them.

Parts of the main north-south highway in Oriental Mindoro had no asphalt and the dust rose up behind us in a wide plume, which, whenever the driver had to brake, would cover us all with a choking cloud as fine as talcum powder. The glassless windows were just open apertures which could be closed with a wooden screen coming up from a recess at the window's base if shade was required instead of view. You soon became accustomed to travelling everywhere with a large handkerchief, which, besides being useful for mopping your brow, could cover your mouth whenever the driver braked or when a vehicle passed.

The "ductors', as the conductors were familiarly referred to, in a sort of playful way, elevating them to the like-sounding title of 'doctor', were men who had a phenomenal propensity to memorise everyone's fares. Rather than the apparently simpler method of charging on issuing the tickets, the 'ductor would issue the tickets first then collect the fares later. These tickets were personalised for every passenger's requirements, the 'ductor rapidly perforating the complex grids of squares printed on his ticket book, using a deftly-handled clipper. The precise kilometre along the route where you had boarded the bus and the kilometre where you were to disembark were appropriately punched out. It must have taken hours memorising all the distances of every village, road junction and public building. The clipping-out of date, distance and fare deposited over the passengers a fine snow of paper circles.

Having issued all the tickets, the 'ductor collected the fares, rarely asking anyone to repeat their destination, and having already calculated the fare – even the amount involving multiple fares. He folded the paper notes in half lengthways, each denomination kept separate from the other and wrapped around an assigned finger and with the note ends splaying out, made his hand look as though it was carrying some kind of fan. The coins simply went into his jeans' pocket, but often he kept a piso coin, which owing to its diameter could be snugly secured in the folds of an ear, for that quicker transaction of change requiring a piso.

You didn't have to wait for a bus stop in order to get down but the driver or 'ductor's attention could be summoned in one of several ways. The passenger could shout, *'Para ho!'* or alternatively it was quite in order to make a loud, very squeaky-sounding kissing noise that seemed quite outrageously suggestive except to a Filipino! If your voice was drowned by engine sounds, with the hurricane rush of wind obliterating all but the shrillest or lustiest of voices, it was customary to rap your knuckles on the hardboard ceiling and yell out *'Para ho!'* This was relayed down to the front by several helpful passengers – those closest to the driver blowing a rasping kiss. The 'ductor would often add to this signal by striking a piso coin or his ticket hole puncture against one of the hollow steel grab-poles positioned along the bus corridor.

The 'ductors were usually very friendly individuals, steadying you by the arm (done with gusto for the young ladies) when coming on and off the bus, since it was easy to topple over at such speeds on Mindoro's potholed roads. An added difficulty involved negotiating a course around everyone's bags and the sacks of merchandise that cluttered the aisle. The 'ductors also helped to pass your luggage down. I always felt that such men with their cheerful capacity to serve, always looking out for the needs of others, together with their undoubted intelligence, were made of the very stuff needed for the running of the country.

We arrived in Bongabong shortly after eight in the morning. Bob and Joy Hanselman rented a large

Jeepney fording the Batangan River
John Richards

semi-detached house, whilst the other half of the semi was used as a rice store. This attracted many rats. The barrenness of their home impressed us. The Hanselmans kept their few belongings secured inside one trunk and a suitcase, both of which were suspended by lengths of rope dangling from ceiling hooks in order to outwit the rats! After breakfast, we travelled together to the plaza to board the jeepney which would take us toward our Buhid village: destination – Batangan.

The jeepney we boarded was no wonder of popular art as typically found in Manila and provincial capitals. Its dull brown/red paint had almost vanished, looking as though it had been burnt off in a fire, which to judge by appearances had happened when the vehicle had somersaulted down a hillside before bursting into flame. The upholstery on the seats was excessively torn, the foam exposed in places and largely missing elsewhere from the wooden bench seats, persuading us to sit on the wood. The exposed foam was often soggy from un-nappied babies and children.

On such trips into remote places, jeepneys are filled way beyond capacity. Smaller children are seated on parents' laps and larger ones have to squat down in the central aisle. Sometimes the narrowest of wooden benches is placed down the middle aisle to form a third row, inhibiting the space for knees and feet. Not only is the rear half-door sat on by two people, but many men ride on the roof, perched as best they can upon and around the merchandise placed up there.

Along both sides of the jeepney runs a ledge, two to three centimetres wide, upon which a man can just perch his toes. This provides additional standing room for the daredevils, among whom I became numbered in the course of time. Far from being comfortable, the toes soon began to ache, even to alarmingly shake, when toe muscles have not been used to such precarious perching. Riding in such a preposterous position is made possible only with the positioning of a handrail running down either side of the rooftop, gripped with grim determination and a growing faith in God.

But riding on the outside has its advantages. The view for one thing can be enjoyed, something which is difficult to see from within, as the window level is too low for foreigners who are usually half a head taller than provincial Filipinos, when seated. With the positioning of the additional bench in the central aisle, you cannot stretch your legs and therefore have to slump to avoid your head being squashed at an angle against the ceiling. I attribute my going prematurely thin on my crown to constantly having the top of my head thrust too often against the roof in this manner!

In spite of the sunburn which would probably be worse if it were not for the liberal coating of dust applied, it is exhilarating to ride on the outside with the wind in your face keeping the perspiration at bay for once. Riding on the ledge, living on the very edge, was preferable to the stifling interior of an overcrowded jeepney.

But such foolish prowess is nothing compared with the agility shown by the 'ductor. As collecting fares is generally not possible from within the passenger compartment when the jeepney is full of people and merchandise, the 'ductor walks the ledge around the outside, tapping those within from behind to collect their money. This walk along the outside of the speeding jeep is complicated by the longer-than-desirable stride needed to pass across the broad wheel arch where the ledge disappears. The presence of passengers perched along this ledge does not deter the 'ductor, either, from doing these rounds, as he is practised at confidently straddling every passenger, passing around on the outside. It is somewhat unpleasant to have to root through your pockets with one hand for the fare, leaving the other to grip with steely, grim determination your only real secure point of contact on this speeding, lurching jeep.

When the 'ductor reaches the front end of the ledge, he will sometimes slip in between the driver and his door for a chat, that is if no one is already sitting there. This place is usually reserved for a pretty girl, enlivening what is an all-too-often travelled route for the driver! The 'ductor completes his tour down the other side by walking over the bonnet as the jeepney hurtles past the flashing greenery of the jungle.

Such journeying improved one's prayer life! Since returning to Scotland, public transport has exerted nothing like the same appeal. Although banning such antics is safer, life loses much of its colour and variety through an abundance of regulations.

The jeepney once made a detour to attend a local cockfight. One of the men strutting along in his dyed vest with a cockerel under his arm, approached a breastfeeding Buhid tribal woman. Muttering something to her, the woman, after a moment's hesitation, nodded at the Tagalog whom she knew. The man proffered his cockerel at the jeepney's window whereupon the woman removing her breast from her infant, pointed it at the bird, squeezing a jet of copious milk onto its head. This unusual anointing seemingly performed some good luck blessing and the cock went on to win the fight. Not all the passengers carrying fighting cocks were so fortunate. One man returned half an hour later clutching a dead fighter by its legs, dejectedly going home with the poor consolation of cooking the tough old bird for dinner.

On this occasion, the jeepney terminated at a collapsed bridge. The passengers had to proceed on foot across a stony waste of a river flood plain over to a makeshift bridge. Hannah hesitated before stepping on to the rickety bridge, and before I had time to rearrange what I was carrying to free an arm to pick her up, a young man called Moses lifted her on to one shoulder and balanced by a huge sack of rice on the other, they crossed the bridge.

Another jeepney took us further on, dropping us off at the next river valley. As we walked up the river valley to Batangan, we occasionally heard an alimahon bird with a deep-throated call like a dense liquid being poured slowly from a narrow-necked bottle; 'bluub-blu-blu-blu-bluub'. Unremarkable in appearance, like so many birds with a thrilling voice, the alimahon resembles a grey dove both in size and shape, with a small russet bib.

Never had we heard sounds like it, rich and exotic, which more than anything, spoke of the foreignness of our surroundings. It had the effect of suddenly and briefly transporting us away from all that was familiar, into a fantasy world.

Later in the day, under the shade of a large mango tree, we sat chatting with Buhid. We had a happy gaggle about us, asking Roberto (as Bob was known to them) and Ligaya (a direct translation of Joy's name in Tagalog) our names and our plans. They customarily asked these questions of a third party. On asking their names, they smiled, looking down at the ground, or turned away. A companion would reply for them but only after an awkward pause. Soon we learned to ask, 'What's your friend's name?' as they showed more ease responding in this manner.

'Nick was a forester from Canada,' began Hagan, an elderly man, with a single tooth remaining in the front of his mouth. His hair was steely grey, very thick for his years. Stiffened by dust, the hair rose of its own accord. It flowed from his head as though the wind blew through it, creating an image of a hale and hearty farmer, running down a mountainside. He laughed at the reminiscence he wished to share before blurting out the anecdote in short blasts, punctuated by more stifled laughter.

'Nick was very good at gathering all the young ones. He had them playing many games, some with Bible questions and others that demanded a feat of skill or even daring. He would separate the young ones into two groups on either side of a river and would place a long thick rope between them. They took the rope up, and then tried to pull the group on the opposite bank into the river! The braver ones he made crouch up inside a truck's tyre and sent them off rolling down a hillside!'

Hagan could no longer go on, if he had more to say, for the recollection of it all had him wheezing with laughter. This made those about him laugh, amused as much by his own bronchial cheer as by the stories he related.

Commonly five foot two or three at best, some adults even under the five-foot mark, they could nevertheless carry huge loads of wood or vast quantities of bananas balanced on either end of a pole. Almost without exception, all were dressed poorly in badly ripped and stained clothes. Those who did not have a torn top stood out from the rest. Most went bare foot although a few wore rubber flip-flops, some repaired with twine; their soles, worn paper-thin, were holed at the main pressure points. Many picked out lice from their neighbour's hair, not in the least perturbed by the problem, since everyone was afflicted alike. Some eventually drifted away after satisfying their curiosity; others, clearly enjoying the shy repartee, lingered on, joined by those coming home from their land with large woven field baskets carried on their backs, secured by a bark strap across the forehead. Some women came with baskets as large as their torsos, filled with yams, cassava, beans still in their pods and the green tops of hot peppers from which to make a watery stew, flavoured with ginger and garlic.

Dusk came swiftly and our group broke up to attend to the evening meal. We cooked a vegetable stew of the many sweet potatoes, beans and leaf tops brought to us earlier, on a paraffin primus stove set upon a grubby and much-dented metal shelf to the side of a sink. Yaba and Mahonay – a couple in their early thirties – turned up to help check the translation work Joy was working on. Not only late in cooking our meal, but later still in eating it, this couple would not partake of anything, insisting they had eaten already. Sitting down with Joy at one end of a long mahogany table, the rest of us quietly ate, not wanting to disrupt the meticulous work of translation checking.

After some time, a man in his early forties drifted in quietly, his moustache and gaunt cheeks twitching as he spoke with Bob in furtive tones.

'We have visitors from the hills – just arrived earlier!'

'Where are they staying?' asked Bob.

'At the other side of town. They are many! It is better that you don't go out again tonight and if anyone comes to your door later on, don't open it!'

'Do they know we're here?'

'Sure they know – they know all such things!' the gaunt man ruffled his slightly curly hair and laughed nervously, his eyes suddenly lustrous in the light of the storm lantern.

'Then we had better be off in the morning – first thing,' remarked Bob.

'You could stay for the church service tomorrow and a few of us could guide you out straight afterwards!'

Bob considered the proposition for a short while.

'No – it would be better if we got clear away early on to lessen the chance of meeting with those from the hills!'

Now looking us over for the first time since entering the room, the moustached man asked, 'What are our friends' names?' The curly-headed fellow pursed his lips briefly in our direction in a friendly gesture, but a quite unnecessary one considering he knew everyone else present.

'They speak Tagalog...' And Bob proceeded to introduce us and explained a little about the reason for our visit.

'And this is Macarios...' Bob said turning to us. He was interrupted.

'My name is Yan-yan!' the other said boldly, taking over the introduction in a manner that was not typical of his timid people. 'Are you coming to live with us?'

'Yes maybe – we very much hope so!' I replied. Yan-yan's smile beamed in the direction of everyone present, making any comment of our being welcome quite superfluous.

'And when can you come?' Yan-yan boldly ventured, now much more animated than he had been during the furtive conversation earlier.

'We are still at language school.' Yan-yan's face perceptibly fell. 'But in two or three months' time we will be moving to Mindoro!' This added news drew out another beaming smile.

'So you will come and live with us then?' Yan-yan asked hopefully.

'Not immediately,' I returned, aware that my explanations were going to dampen his enthusiasm again. 'We will live in one of the towns first, for after we finish our learning at the language school, our studies will go on for probably another year while at the same time we help one of the local churches down on the plains.'

'A year!' Yan-yan's eyebrows shot up in the air. After a second or two of thoughtfully nodding his head, he philosophically remarked, 'After a year you will be better prepared to come and live with us!' He stayed a while longer to finish his coffee and left in a brisk manner.

'Who was that?' Alexandra asked, intrigued.

'Macarios is the Buhid's elected representative on the board of the Mangyan Tribal Church Association. He is often out of town, up in Calapan or even further afield for he is also partly responsible for a non-government organisation that has set up an agricultural programme in the Buhid area. They also undertake to legally register everyone's tribal land, measuring it to acquire land titles.'

'Why did he say his name was Yan-yan if it is Macarios?' I asked.

'Yan-yan is his real name but I introduced him to you as Macarios as Buhid prefer to use their lowland name with outsiders. They are shy to reveal their tribal identity with those they don't know.' Bob paused a moment and went on to remark, 'The fact he used his tribal name meant he felt comfortable with you!'

'And tell us about what he came to say to you in the first place.'

'Yes, I was just coming to that.' Bob shifted uneasily on the bench. 'The NPA arrived earlier and we need to leave at first light before we come across them!' (The NPA – the New People's Army – are a Communist rebel group active in upland Mindoro and other parts of the undeveloped archipelago.)

'What would happen if we met them?'

'They might demand money, belongings...' Bob paused and, looking us in the face, added, 'They might be tempted to kidnap us and hold out for a big ransom on account of our being American!'

Chapter Five:

In Ka Carmen's Back Yard

'Oh, that was great!' shouted Iain, as he careered on his bicycle into the yard into which Alexandra and Hannah had just hurried. There had been another 'aftershock', following an earthquake just a few days earlier, of such force that the track where Iain had been cycling had rippled, providing a fairground ride sensation.

It had not been so pleasant for me. Seated on the toilet, I watched with horror the tiled walls of our tiny bathroom visibly breathing in and out. The ceramic toilet pedestal became suddenly animated as though I were on horse-back, as the ripples passed through the ground. I had thought, 'Not now Lord – I don't want to die with my trousers down, sat here!' I had nobler notions of exiting this world, of at least being attacked by Communist rebels, or of falling into a ravine on my way to reaching a remote mountain village. I was prepared to die, but not under these circumstances!

We had not long moved home from Batangas, across the water to Mindoro and were settled into a ground floor, two-bedroom, mid-terraced row of four other identical units. We considered the accommodation very small, the floor area of the entire house being smaller than a large-sized lounge in a British home. The furniture we had reckoned on fitting in, did not, and some had to be returned to the mission's stores. Whilst there might have been cause to be envious of other colleagues with more spacious accommodation, we were still doing all right by our neighbours' standards. One household at the terrace end squeezed seven children into an identical-sized place. Like many rural Filipinos, they did not bother with beds but slept on mats that during the day were stored away.

A small town on the north-south highway of Oriental Mindoro, the Victoria townsfolk welcomed their first foreigners in many a year, wanting to know why we had come to their rather insignificant town. Now having a reasonable grasp of Tagalog, we didn't disappoint Filipinos so much when they wanted to get to know us. Here we served a one-and-a-half-year apprenticeship, working under a Filipino pastor, learning to do things in a culturally sensitive way and not steamroll in with our foreign ideas.

Away in Manila when the main earthquake shook Oriental Mindoro province, we came back to damage, but nothing like on the scale our neighbours had experienced, where whole cabinets and shelves had ejected their contents onto the floor. This surprised us, particularly since our home faced the same direction as the others and therefore bore the same brunt and force of shock waves as their homes had done. This led our neighbours to earnestly observe that our prayers must be effective – a conclusion we had no part in contriving.

The earthquake had been around 4.7 on the Richter scale, causing minimal collapse of masonry although many building structures were significantly cracked and doors had jammed. The major loss of life was caused by the resultant tsunami, laying bare a whole half-mile or more of ocean floor as the sea retreated towards an outlying island just around the point from Calapan (where the epicentre was). The ten-foot wave, deflected by the two offshore islands, had missed Calapan but its roar had awakened those housed close to the shore, making them run for higher ground. The tsunami had struck the coast a few miles further on, lifting the floating power barge and thrusting it a mile inland. Children unable to swim or withstand the beating against debris and vegetation, were killed. Some corpses were even brought down from overhead branches where they had been drowned.

The earth tremors also caused liquefaction. One such pool, appearing right outside the Catholic Church in Calapan, became a centre of superstitious pilgrimage for a while, once the waters were pronounced 'holy' and to have possible healing qualities.

There had also been a number of landslides. A hillside had slipped into a valley, just into the hills near to Victoria, damming the river and causing a substantial lake to form. The military were particularly evident, making helicopter sorties from the town hall to view this new lake. Like many others, I went to the town hall to learn the news and hear the advice.

'The lake is seven bamboo lengths in depth,' one soldier informed the crowd, a depth probably in the region of 150 feet.

'Is the dam going to burst?' asked one frightened young woman. The soldier paused before shrugging his shoulders. Panic gripped the town of Victoria, downstream from this dam. One or two people were evacuating the area fearing an imminent deluge should this frail dam burst.

'Are you going to desert us too?' asked one small girl a few minutes later, as we walked home close by to her shanty house. Her eyes were large with fear, realising her own helplessness. It was that appeal, combined with the appearance of many children at our door shortly afterwards, which made us decide to stay and show solidarity with those who had nowhere to move to and no financial means either to evacuate en masse. We prayed with them, asking God to give us courage as well as requesting him to avert this potential disaster. 'After all,' Alexandra concluded, 'this is one reason why we are here in the Philippines, to show courage and faith at such a time as this!'

We had a great sense of peace, of having made the right choice. The calmness with which the children departed from our house after praying, learning that we would remain with them, also confirmed the appropriateness of this decision.

The authorities were sending out mixed advice.

That night we prepared an emergency bag packed with identity papers, a torch, money, an umbrella, drinking water and photograph negatives (the latter, my wife's compromise to avoid carrying the many photo albums). We were at a loss to know what else might be useful or appropriate in the event of a deluge! We also made a contingency plan about how we were going to climb up onto the roof of our landlady's tall house.

The disaster never struck. A day or two later, a team of engineers and workers opened up a channel to divert the waters into a neighbouring river, draining off the lake.

Within the first few days of our moving in to our new home, Iain slipped on the wet tiles of our bathroom floor and gashed his head open. As with the manner of head wounds, it bled prolifically despite efforts to stem the flow. This event helped us in getting to know our neighbours as we approached them, asking directions for the health clinic. Pong, a truck driver and our immediate neighbour, said he would take us there in the landlady's 'owner jeep'.

'Just give me a minute whilst I ask Ka Carmen for the jeep's keys.' He reappeared a few minutes later with another young man – 'Piping' – who went about in a vest permanently rolled up over his barrelled belly. Proud of its considerable proportions, he was keen to display it, indicating he was a man of means and of leisure. Piping's wife worked in Italy as a domestic helper and provided for her family with the transmissions she sent home. These two men very attentively led our family to the owner jeep. Gates had to be opened and the vehicle needed a push start after a few failed attempts with the ignition. We were off, holding a reddening towel to Iain's head. All this activity – the ride in the back of a jeep and getting acquainted with these new neighbours – helped take our minds off the alarming injury. The clinic, proving to be in the next street, would have been more quickly reached had we walked there! Nevertheless, we appreciated their concern and practical help.

Iain was attended to immediately. Made to sit on a stretcher bed on wheels (the PVC covering of which was all split and stained with old blood), our son looked intently about him, absorbing so much of this new experience that he forgot about his wound. The doctor cleaned the wound with hydrogen peroxide, which sprayed with a fascinating fizz and a momentary, expanding effervescence. Filipino doctors are experts at stitching for they regularly have to stitch men up after knife fights – the frequent result of drinking parties when passions have been raised after gambling at cards.

Iain and Hannah now mixed well with the lowland Filipino children, moving on from Batangas and from the difficulties encountered with some of the neighbours there. The new place provided a fresh start, and we were more aware now of the cultural nuisances and more able to avoid the unintentional blunders. But life was still full of the interesting interactions of two cultures.

Hannah persuaded one lad, slightly younger than her, to smear one of her concoctions consisting of a ground-up leaf paste over parts of his face where he would like hair to grow, 'Because if you do,' suggested Hannah, 'you will have a beard like my daddy's!' This, the young lad dutifully did, smearing copious amounts across his jaw much to the furious consternation of his mother. 'Dong' was her name. Her preoccupation, like that of most Filipina mothers, was to ensure her children were presentable, so they would not be derided as street urchins. More unfortunate for the young lad was the resultant rash that erupted across his face as a result of this leaf concoction.

Dong, who incidentally was Pong's wife, had once tried to discipline Hannah. Her small apartment was the servants' quarters in the home of her landlady, who was also her godmother. The home was connected by an unlocked adjoining door, enabling the godmother-landlady to ask various favours of Dong. Hannah, being a curious five-year-old, wanted to know what was on the other side of this door. Dong indulgently allowed her to look around the home of the absent godmother, but drew the line when Hannah wanted to explore upstairs. 'There is a ghost up there,' cautioned Dong in the usual manner Filipinos adopt to curb a child's curiosity.

'Oh good,' responded Hannah, 'I have never seen a ghost before!' upon which Hannah went striding briskly upstairs in hope of an encounter. Later Dong confided her surprise over Hannah's fearlessness! How on earth did we manage to restrain our children 'if they were unafraid of ghosts'?

Our landlady lived just across the yard. Ka Carmen Gaod worked in the town hall, overseeing the various elections that took place with surprising frequency on national, provincial and even at municipal levels. Ka Carmen was protective of us, glad of the prestige foreigners brought – *Amerikanos* – renting one of her apartments. Her husband had spent many years working in Saudi Arabia, earning the money to build their substantial house and the five rented apartments. Ka

Rolly – as the husband was known – still worked in the Middle East at the time of our coming to Victoria and since Ka Carmen could not drive, she sometimes called upon me to chauffeur her about in her owner jeep. The owner jeep was locally made from gleaming panels of chrome, and sections of unpainted, lustreless steel, finished off with a canvas top and sides. The 'owner' had tiny side doors, less than a foot in height; they did not keep the rain out, but rather provided a bare modicum of privacy, shielding the view of the lower half of the body seated low in seats raised barely above floor level. With a jeep-like front, it was the sort of vehicle one imagines driving on a beach; designed for fun, for the short outing, rather than for covering any serious distance.

Driving her slowly about town, Ka Carmen would sit up front in the passenger seat whilst the rest of my family squeezed on to the bench-like back seat, enjoying the novelty of travelling about in a private vehicle. Ka Carmen sat there permanently thrilled, scanning the road before her, shouting out greetings to every friend and acquaintance, pulling back the side canvas flaps and waving an arm with gusto to ensure she was noticed, regally driven by her foreign chauffeur! Having a white person chauffeuring her about made her laugh with delight and literally she clapped her hands together from time to time in an expression of sheer joyful intoxication. All the while she talked with a strident voice which needed no amplification even if she were to address a vast crowd. She spoke at quite a speed and had our minds spinning, trying to decipher her exclamations of delight mixed in with information about the people she saw and the last-second directions all said with a single breath as if it were but one sentence.

'But I can't turn left down here,' I once protested, 'there's a no-entry sign!'

Ka Carmen blew out her cheeks and waved a hand dismissively at the sign. 'Those signs are for foreigners only!' she said in all earnestness. After a moment's reflection she slapped my arm and loudly exclaimed with intense mirth, 'And you're a foreigner! It's for you!' She laughed a good half-minute, amused by how preposterously foreigners obeyed a dull symbol painted on a little sign. She was quite right in a way, for there were hardly any other private vehicles in this provincial town and this route was not used by public jeepneys. Once she had composed herself, she commanded me to drive down the one-way street and, taking hold of the wheel, she gave it a good yank round, making it quite clear that she was to be obeyed. 'We're Filipino!' she laughingly declared. We did not meet anyone coming the other way and even if we had, it would not have been a problem since there was adequate passing space.

Bonfire night came up in our school curriculum and we decided to mark the occasion, not only out of our duty to educate our children in the eccentricity of this occasion, but with a degree of sought-after nostalgia. We purchased some fireworks from the market but drew the line at making a guy, showing our children instead a picture of a burning effigy illustrated in the school course-book. Our explanations of Guy Fawkes night to Ka Carmen, Dong, Pong and the other neighbours were met with blank expressions. They were quite taken aback, unsure how to react to foreigners who celebrated an attempt to blow up their own government building and commemorated the occasion by raising an effigy of the chief culprit to burn at the stake. This information contradicted their picture of the civilised west, making them consider that perhaps we came from some barbaric part of the States (of which they insisted Britain was a part).

The fireworks were large items, hand-wrapped in bright gift-wrap paper, without a single instruction or trademark. I appeased my safety concerns with the observation that all had ample lengths of blue touchpaper providing plenty of time, once lit, to retire to a suitable distance. There was a problem though; the blue touchpaper, not really being too combustible, repeatedly went out. The length grew shorter and shorter until I resorted to screwing up a sheet of newspaper beside the first firework and lighted the paper hoping it would in turn ignite the firework. A huge explosive blast from the first firework brought all the remaining neighbours running out of their houses, happily curious to inquire as to what was going on. Fireworks in the Philippines are associated with the New Year season and even though festive seasons in the Philippines are far more fluid as to when they actually begin and end, November was really still too early for firecrackers.

Christmas was soon upon us, with the carolling season beginning in early December. Every night a large crowd of the neighbourhood youngsters gathered outside our home, regaling us with their shouty songs, hoping for a handout of a few pisos at the end. Well prepared for this by placing all our coin change in a pot for a couple of weeks now, we meant to avoid the embarrassment of the previous year when we ran short too soon. Before long we began to recognise some of the carollers' faces, realising these were the same ones returning night after night, keen to milk us dry! It was Dong and Pong who sent them away eventually.

Bimbo (a lad of Iain's age who had the misfortune to be given this 'dumb blonde' name which held no such connotations to Filipinos) and his sister Cherry-Loot – as her name Charlotte was pronounced – decided to go carolling too. A lad called Bok-bok – a nickname meaning weevil on account of his slight frame and its amazing elasticity – joined them. Not having the audacity to repeatedly go to the foreigners' home and somewhat unhappy about the little they received elsewhere, they persuaded us to allow Iain and Hannah to join them. Their fortunes soon began to rise. Noticing how Iain and Hannah were the ones usually to be given the money (which subsequently they shared around the group) the worldly-wise Bimbo, Cherry-Loot and Bok-bok positioned them at the front to be easily spotted in the darkness. The group's major asset of white faces and the smiling blue eyes, considered 'so cute', was used for maximum advantage on all adoring Filipinos! It worked wonders, exciting a generosity unprecedented in Victoria at Christmases before.

The children of one family were generally excluded from any game or carolling. They had constructed a lean-to shack of old timber and worn corrugated roofing sheets, against the concrete wall of an immense storeroom built opposite Ka Carmen's fine house. They were the only squatter family in our part of the street. One of their daughters – Marie-Sel – having a shaven head to rid her of lice, had been given a red sun hat with two plaited skeins of black wool in imitation of hair plaits, dangling down either side. The other children made sport of her, creeping up behind to whisk away the hat with the hair attachments, to mock her bald head. Marie-Sel never cried, at least not in the street. She boldly held back the tears standing in her eyes, knowing she would be derided mercilessly should a tear fall! Her brother showed no such restraint, quickly gaining a reputation for wildly lashing out as he fought for his rights. Unfortunately this only led the others to bait him to get the desired reaction. All such families are considered undesirable and not always without reason since their precarious existence could push them towards illegal ways.

The neighbourhood turned a blind eye to all this teasing and bullying unless Marie-Sel's wild brother succeeded in hitting one of his taunters! Then he would be severely reprimanded by the injured child's parent. The lad would then be beaten indoors by parents desperate to be no longer maligned, despairing about being blamed for everything that was wrong. Iain and Hannah though reacted strongly against such teasing and baiting, standing up for Marie-Sel in particular. Hannah made Marie-Sel's hat no longer the source of ridicule when she had Alexandra sew two plaited skeins of yellow wool onto a similar sun hat. Suddenly it became endearing and Marie-Sel was relieved to find herself to be wearing a fashionable garment.

Late afternoon, once the worst of the heat was over, we sat on the low wall running along the side of Ka Carmen's house where a welcome breeze often blew off the nearby paddy fields. As well as overseeing the children, there was opportunity to chat with neighbours glad to have finished the day's many chores. With so many being under one roof, combined with the Tagalog's preoccupation with pristine presentation, laundry seemed an unending task for the majority of households and, without washing machines, laundry at the communal pump was a daily occupation.

When the children's play turned rough, our neighbours were surprised to find us often taking sides with the squatter children, assuming that, not being of that class of people ourselves, we would approve of their being taunted and ousted. Generally respecting their elders, the children heeded our sense of fair play and desisted from such segregational behaviour. We had to be firm and yet tactful in holding our ground with the parents who encouraged their children to isolate Marie-Sel's family. They laughed out of embarrassment at our altruistic ways, yet acknowledged that such ideals were right. They found it hard to put such standards into practice, for this involved unlearning a lifetime of prejudices; yet gradually, we noticed the squatter family became a more accepted part of our immediate community.

Christmas marked the real beginning when Marie-Sel's family became more included. Marie-Sel enjoyed carolling with the Cherry-Loot group and was included in the Christmas party held in Ka Carmen's covered terrace. Dong, having been asked to prepare some games and relying on her husband Pong to help her out, came to us on the morning of the party, distressed that Pong had had to drive a truck up to Manila that morning and asked, could we do the games?

Before the games commenced, the teenagers transformed our kitchen/diner into a stage equipped with microphone, amplifier and speaker. They performed some Karaoke numbers complete with stage routines involving synchronised movements and theatrical arm gestures. For some days they had been rehearsing and what they lacked in singing ability they succeeded in carrying off through sheer confidence. Their delivery was with such earnestness that one felt uncharitable for entertaining any critical thoughts. No wonder they oozed confidence. Even the four- or five-year-olds were encouraged and cajoled into taking up the mike and trotting out their favourite numbers.

As soon as their lengthy repertoire had finished, the games began with unabated enthusiasm. Young and old were determined to make this day like no other; a day that would be elevated in their memories like an imposing monument that rose high above the ordinariness of their hum-drum existence. With the

Filipino's love of party games we had by this time accumulated quite a repertoire (in comparison with their own), and knew the ones especially appreciated. These included games like the spoon tied to the end of a long string that had to be passed along a line of people forming two competing teams, up and down through everyone's clothing! There were innumerable games involving balloons – balloon volleyball, relay races of jumping with a balloon between your knees and such like. There were other entertainments like Pelmanism, pin the tail on the donkey, musical chairs, all vigorously pursued in a blur of ecstatic smiles and raucous laughter.

Those who could not join in some game because of the limit on numbers, pushed and elbowed just to be able to look on at what was generally regarded as extraordinary. Even the men came to gawk, temporarily foregoing their intent of getting well and truly sozzled (on a day when they did not much run the risk of being chastised by their wives, since the occasion afforded a certain allowance for excesses – even an expectation!). They amused everyone by their inept attempts in the advanced stages of inebriation to compete stupidly in a game of eating an apple suspended from a string, without the aid of hands.

Hosting the Noche Buena – the feast eaten at midnight as Christmas Eve merges into Christmas Day – Ka Carmen had prepared the greater share of the dishes. These were handsomely supplemented by contributions from all the other neighbours. After four hours of games, we managed to persuade everyone that our repertoire was exhausted and with a second repetition, the favourites would perhaps begin to lose their appeal. We finally enjoyed resting on Ka Carmen's spacious terrace, mostly seated on the low marble slab-topped wall.

Photocopied sheets combining Tagalog and English carols were heartily sung to my accompaniment on a guitar. These Roman Catholic families had accepted us Protestants, realising we had much in common in matters of faith when focusing on Christ rather than on his mother. A great sense of bonhomie carried us on together; we were experiencing the same religious thrill as we sang more from the heart, the initial reserve melting away as the awe of that first Christmas became more apparent.

Sometime around midnight, just at the close of the singing and after a prayer, Ka Carmen suddenly stood up and clapped her hands for attention, a quite superfluous action since we were all quiet anyway. Ka Carmen liked a sense of occasion, permitting her to be just that bit more flamboyant. She looked regal in her long, cream Spanish gown, embellished with pleats and darts, with a bodice encrusted with imitation pearls. She was officiating at the handing out of the exchange presents. (These were distributed but none opened, since that was considered bad form, lest a vague disappointment be perceived by the giver in the expression of the receiver.) Ka Carmen Gaod disappeared indoors, emerging with the ingratiating smile of a games show hostess, holding up high a huge orange fan fashioned from crisp 20 piso notes. She paused, speechless, her deliberate delay producing an anticipated tension over what was to happen next. She wafted herself with the rich fan. To each child she gave one note. Ken – the lad who had smeared his face with leaf paste – ran up out of turn to collect his gift.

'You share this one with your sister,' commanded Ka Carmen, handing a single note to the crestfallen lad. Much to our embarrassment, she gave Iain and Hannah five 20 piso notes each! Uncomfortable with the extravagant favour and spurred by a sense of injustice, they later each gave Ken 20 pisos, making him considerably better off than his peers. The night was rounded off with a huge banquet buffet. We all went off, bloated, to bed.

The Christmas party had been such a success that the whole neighbourhood insisted on repeating the entire programme the following week on New Year's Eve. Another banquet was laid out at Ka Carmen's with each household providing their fair share. Under the grand lady's instigation, there was to be dancing out in the yard; there was even to be a competition for various dances and age categories. We were somewhat apprehensive about what Ka Carmen would have us do as she was fond of Latin dancing and attended classes every Thursday night at the town hall – to which she had unsuccessfully tried persuading Alexandra. When dressed in her flamboyant Spanish gown, I had misgivings that her pièce de résistance would be having the *Amerikano* do the tango with her in front of a sizeable crowd!

All these fears were quite unfounded for Ka Carmen only had disco music in mind and she established herself as the judge. No sooner had the beat of the music struck up than all the Filipino children were body-popping, feet fixed to the spot, with their bodies flexing at every conceivable joint. Some mysterious force appeared to come up through the concrete activating them with switch-like immediacy, propelling them into considerable motion, to express the beat's alluring quality. They excelled, particularly Bok-bok, who true to his nickname, 'the weevil', had an elasticity incredible to behold. Our children won a prize each, more out of the hostess's graciousness than any innate expertise on their part.

The night had been another complete success – although the majority of men segregated themselves from the rest of the party, sitting in some dingy side alley around a table laden with bottles of beer, gin and rum, chewing on the bones of a stray dog killed earlier and barbecued. As we shut up house that night, Alexandra called me over to the window.

'Look at Pong!' she sniggered.

The very much worse-for-wear truck driver was busy trying to find the door to his house. He was looking for it where it had formerly been a few months earlier, and had since been blocked up. His hands ran along the length of the wall intent on finding the frame. He stopped, scratched his head and ran his hands back along the wall again to where he had started at the corner. He stood there half a minute, swaying, apparently wondering how his home had lost its front door. At that moment, Dong emerged from the new entrance round the corner.

'Come in here, you drunken fool!' Pong staggered forward throwing his arms around his wife and the two of them clumsily disappeared from view into the house.

The festive season passed and the dull routine of life resumed once again, balancing teaching Iain and Hannah with helping to run the local church, and progressing with our own cultural studies in the final approach to the completion of our formal Tagalog studies.

Lito and Libay, a young couple who owned a corner shop, said we could go and work through our assignments with them over the slack period during the hottest part of the day – between two to four in the afternoon. From them, we learned how a boy courts the favour of a girl, usually with the boy making a reference to their possibly going out together but almost always in the guise of a flippant remark, which could be construed as a joke, to make the proposition easier to reject without the lad losing face. We studied what qualities men looked for in a prospective bride and vice versa, noting that Filipinos have a far less romantic criterion than westerners do – the imperative in both cases being the most practical one of the girl being well domesticated and numerate to manage the household's accounts and the boy hard working, able to hold down a job. A balanced character was far more important than either looks or a sense of fun.

It was curious, too, noting what people bought from their shop. Cigarettes were sold individually and lit by a lighter suspended from a string hung from the light. Finger slim polythene bags of cooking oil, salt, monosodium glutamate and individual sachets of hair shampoo and conditioner were bought as often people did not have the money to buy what westerners would regard as standard-sized merchandise. Even magazines were rented by the day rather than bought; comic-strips written for an adult market, romances and horror and violent action being the most popular, were carefully selected before paying the piso rental. One day I picked up one of these to pass the time whilst Lito and Libay were serving customers.

I read a comic strip explaining why Filipinos had flat noses. A grandmother explained that in the beginning God made people without noses. The caption showed a variety of very flat-faced people going about their business. Then one day God decided to rain down noses from the heavens. Overjoyed to select a beautiful nose for themselves, people rushed to select the most admirable-looking shapes and sizes, but those who were lazy were only left with the noses that had been squashed underfoot!

'We don't like our noses!' Libay explained with a snigger, holding her own nose in her hand as though hiding it from our view. 'Your nose is much more beautiful, for it's large and pointed!' This in turn made me consciously touch my own nose.

'Our movie stars spend fortunes to get a special nose job done,' Lito expanded, citing the names of a few of the stars of the Filipino cinema who had had the plastic surgeons narrow their nostrils and add an extension.

'That's ridiculous,' laughed my wife. 'My stepsister had an operation to reduce the size of her nose!'

'Why would she want to do that?' the couple responded with genuine incredulity. We agreed that no one was satisfied with their own looks.

I recall a Japanese student at the language school who admired an Irish girl's prominent nose.

'May I touch it?' the Japanese girl asked and without waiting for the answer lest she be refused, she lent across the jeepney we were travelling in, and in front of everyone, tweaked the Irish girl's nose.

'I don't believe you just did that!' exclaimed the Irish girl shaking her head with disbelief, whilst the Japanese girl sat back with the satisfied look of a lifetime's dream fulfilled.

'If I were to become pregnant again,' announced Ka Carmen to us one day, 'I would look at Iain and Hannah all day long!' We asked why, and she explained, 'Because the child in your womb takes on the resemblance of the one you admire most and spend time looking at during pregnancy!'

'I think there might be some explaining to do if you ever had a white baby!' I remarked. Not understanding my remark, she pressed me to elaborate, until I regretted having made any comment. She thought this suggestion was preposterous, although the suspicion would be quite obvious with her husband still working in Saudi Arabia.

We were into the third year of home-schooling Iain and Hannah. The joy of being together longer was far greater than our disappointment over the consequences of being slower passing through the language course.

Academically, our children seemed to be doing well. But we still had nagging concerns as to how well they were really performing, compared with their own cultural peers, and truly wondered if we were not being just a little irresponsible! In hindsight these fears were totally groundless, but at the time they were inflated by an over-conscientious concern to provide a decent education, and our questioning whether we as parent-teachers were what was best for them.

During our short stay in Singapore we had visited a former tea plantation owner's house up in the Cameron Highlands that had become Chefoo School. This school provided primary education for the children of the mission throughout South East Asia. The temperate-like climate and natural surroundings provided an ideal place for young children to grow up in a safe and healthy environment. Chefoo School was run like a family. With only 40 children in the care of almost half that number of teaching and dorm staff, we had been impressed by a high standard of care and genuine affection from both adult and child.

The unwanted attention of having white skin and blue eyes naturally drew Filipinos to often play teasingly with our children. This resulted in Iain and Hannah being labelled proud when they did not respond warmly to all the irritating cheek-pinching and the questions asked in the childlike voices some adults would adopt. The occasional touching of the genitalia, not considered in the provinces as sex abuse but a gesture of fondness, we viewed as unacceptable. We knew of one neighbour, who, when drunk, had paedophiliac leanings and children had to be kept away from him. That neighbour's son – Jerk-na-Jerk, as we referred to him (the repetition of the adjective joined by a Tagalog linker word placed emphasis on his characteristic) – had a drink and drug problem and would gravitate towards our children when under the influence because they stood out. More an irritating pest to be watched rather than a proven menace, Jerk-na-Jerk was nevertheless a potential threat. Threats were made during one town fiesta to kidnap our children and hold them for ransom to provide a drinking gang with beer money through the festival weekend. These extraneous factors added to the culture stress normally encountered.

We relented and came to the heartbreaking decision to send Iain and Hannah to Chefoo boarding school in Malaysia.

I do wonder though whether we should not have home-schooled for longer since both children responded well to being taught by us? I think we should have. Even on an academic assessment, they learned more in our situation in Victoria by having to learn to adapt to Filipino culture than in the semi-artificial, hermetic world of a privileged school. First-hand experience of another way of life, an alternative outlook to consider, was most educational. This appraisal of one's own national assumptions challenged the 'our-ways-are-best' kind of mentality, and had something winsome and refreshing about it. Iain and Hannah did learn much from their coming and going into the deprived environment we had chosen to live in, providing a comparison between extremes of east and west, privileged and despised, that made them value more the benefits they enjoyed.

In spite of our misgivings, Iain and Hannah thought boarding school an exciting adventure – 'a holiday without Mummy and Daddy!' as Hannah put it. Much of the school life was just that, as they adventured in the jungle and made dens in a place they called 'Primeval'. Times were occasionally tinged with homesickness in those early years but never, seemingly, on the par that we missed them. We did not express our feelings too much, not wanting to unsettle them. Rather, we buried ourselves in our work to suppress the pain and occupy our minds with other thoughts. The school holidays became hugely important to recover lost time and rediscover the dynamics of family life. The children had an eight-week holiday after every 17-week term, so for two glorious holiday periods in a year, we revelled in being a family; although we were not on holiday ourselves for most of that time, we passed the time imaginatively.

The giving-up of our independence, the selling of a thriving guest house and entering into a stage when we became nobodies, unable to communicate, fairly useless at making a valid contribution at first, were sacrifices made that were nothing in comparison to the pain of parting with our children. Some thought us callous, beyond understanding, but they chose not to see the heartache just below the surface, nor the intellectual struggles of making a decision genuinely based on what we thought was best for our children. And yet through all this turbulent emotion and thought, we all received strength to go through with the plan, and a calm descended upon each that was not of our own making. We hurt but did not fret, as we knew of one even more committed to us than we could ever be committed to one another. In God was our rest!

Chapter Six:

Starting All Over Again

Three years after arriving in the Philippines, we finally moved to live with the Buhid tribe and commence our first real assignment. Three years of preparation involving cultural assimilation, gaining a confidence to speak at a deep and meaningful level in the national Tagalog language, enabled us to finally connect with Filipinos. Three years spent more observing than contributing anything of real worth, avoiding the mistakes and arrogance of past eras when foreign cultures were imported and imposed; preparation without which it would have been too easy to make a church look and feel like one brought from home.

At home with the Buhid in Batangan
Anni Bosch

Ernesto – the Swiss tribal team leader in our organisation – brought us into Batangan in a Nissan pickup truck. We had waited until Iain and Hannah were back from Chefoo to make this important move together, making it a family move and not something done in their absence.

Ernesto and I gathered water from a concrete cistern a couple of hundred yards away. This water tank was the project of an independent aid organisation led by an American who had spent upward of fifteen years in Mindoro prior to our arrival. Kiko had come as a Peace Corps worker, and probably finding it restrictive trying to settle back in the States afterwards, he returned to a worthwhile role, having acquired a penchant for tribal living. Fluent in several Filipino languages, he went native, going about in a G-string and chewing betel nut.

Kiko was an enigma to the 'Luktanon' (a Batangan Buhid term referring to all non-Mangyan Filipinos) who made up wild stories of him having many Mangyan wives, rumours that he played upon, feeding their amazed curiosity with what their itching ears wanted to hear.

'My favourite Mangyan wife is really very old and now quite toothless!' was a typical remark. Kiko seemed content to remain single; his altruistic ways motivated him to aid a powerless people to face and overcome much injustice and prejudice. Several months passed before we met Kiko. Hannah often recalls our first meeting, for walking by my side, she saw him up a tree wearing only a loincloth, whiter than his Buhid companions. She giggled, making the observation, thankfully in a subdued voice, 'Daddy, look! That Buhid man there has a white bottom – and it's hairy!'

Whilst filling our containers, we noticed a blacksmith busy at work nearby under a shady canopy of woven palm fronds. We wandered over.

'*Faduwa-SAY!*' the blacksmith greeted us, emphasising the end syllable and lengthening this into a melodious drawl. Although at the time not understanding this Buhid word for 'brother', the blacksmith's tone was unmistakably welcoming.

'What are you making?' Ernesto asked the man who had surprisingly red lips as though coloured by inferior lipstick. When the blacksmith smiled, his teeth were all red as well, dark red like old meat. He spat on the ground a stream of what looked like blood and pushed something with his tongue into his cheek so as to speak more easily.

'I'm making a *fotol*,' informed the blacksmith, handling the developing blade of a machete with an air of knowing scrutiny. He began to chew on the package in his mouth, a mixture of betel nut and lime that the Buhid are fond of chewing, staining their mouths various shades of anything between red and orange. 'Yes it is going to be a *fotol*, that is what I am making!' The man laughed, crouched down and bounced on his haunches good humouredly as though spring-loaded. He placed the blade back in the glowing charcoal embers. With a long metal poker bent at right angles at the end, he carefully scooped some more burning coals on top of the blade, with the fluid motion of one who went about his daily trade. Another, indifferent to our arrival, squatted on top of a bamboo floor platform, operating the bellows. He wore his hair long, gathered into a ponytail secured by a red and white strip of cloth, which also wound around his forehead. Both the blacksmith and his companion wore only loincloths, a most suitable attire for such hot work in the tropics, but hardly approved safety clothing!

The bellows consisted of two parallel thick bamboo sections cleared of their internal dividing membranes, allowing air to pass down the wide stem before being forced into two narrow bamboo stems set horizontally at the base, to intensify the burning embers. The air was moved by two rods with half a coconut shell on each end, wrapped about with strips of old cloth to create a seal and smooth suction. These rods were driven up and down, soundless except for the air hoarsely blowing on the reddening coals.

'Where are you coming from?' inquired the blacksmith. We told him.

'*Aah faduwaSAAY*, which of you is staying to live here with us?' I smiled, indicating that it was me. At this the blacksmith got all excited and, still resting on his haunches, started to bounce up and down again as though he were a cockerel tied up, trying to fly. Periodically he let out flourishes of what sounded like poetic lines delivered in a sing-song cadence, none of which made any sense as it didn't sound like Tagalog. He eulogised a joy that seemed overstated, all the while maintaining his bouncing posture, interspersed with occasional brief bursts of hand clapping and further expostulations.

His manner was absolutely fascinating. His name was Inggoy, a man we grew to love and appreciate over the coming years for his warmth of character, and eccentric manner – the latter which even caused his fellow tribespeople to smile fondly. He brightened up church meetings with his interruptions, no matter if someone was in a middle of a sermon or making a point in a business meeting. Inggoy would chip in with his winsome smile, his face all screwed up benevolently before he wound himself up with what became his characteristic trademark of bouncing excitedly on his haunches, perched on the edge of a church bench. He would reiterate a point he liked, giving it added emphasis to the whole assembly, or perhaps ask for clarification when he had not quite grasped a matter. He would conclude with a brief summary once he had understood, elongating the syllables in that sing-song way of his as he concluded with a 'tha-a-at's ri-i-ight!' If Inggoy's behaviour was affected, his manner would eventually have become tedious, but never laughing at his own amusing antics, even when the laughter of others was explosive, made us conclude his was pure eccentricity of the most endearing kind.

That evening, the church elders came to our house, with many more besides, to discuss their expectations and to inquire about our needs. Roughly twenty in number, although one or two extra people came and went, we sat on the floor forming a quadrangle, leaning against the wall, with our feet meeting in the centre. Over these darkly tanned, scarred, muscular limbs, a few small children clambered naked except for grubby and torn vests. Mostly men, our guests were very relaxed and natural before foreigners without the formality we had grown so accustomed to in the lowland churches. They were farmers, without airs and graces. Their hands and feet struck me as being so different from our own! Theirs had many layers of skin, callused and cracked, the innumerable layers sometimes splitting so badly as to penetrate right through to the tender flesh.

They were a jovial lot, full of wisecracks, none of which we understood at the time since they spoke in Buhid, quite unintelligible even to anyone fluent in Tagalog. They felt very at home with one another, many leaning shoulder to shoulder with arms draped over a neighbour's shoulder or leg, the majority being blood relatives, the remainder related through marriage. Simply dressed in very old clothes – T-shirts and shorts, torn and stained and none too clean – they came in what they had been wearing earlier in the fields. Whenever we caught their eye they briefly beamed a smile back before looking away abashed, indicating an immense welcome that had no need for words, a welcome so embracing that it seemed we had known them for years. Indeed we had been long destined for this moment, to become part of the tribe.

'So, what is it you would like from Martin and Alexandra, bearing in mind they only have six months remaining before they return to their home country?' asked Ernesto. 'Perhaps you should really consider asking them only one thing because they need time to learn something of your language and culture!'

We cringed to think the learning process was about to begin all over again, frustrating our desire to really give something in return. We so much needed to contribute something for the general good to better motivate our return the following year. If we had started nothing, if we had touched no one's life, we might question the validity of returning.

'We want to grow in Christ!' replied Monay, their main elder. Various others nodded their heads. We were somewhat taken aback; we had become so accustomed to the task-type mentality of the lowland churches, keen to discharge some office of function upon us. The Buhid had true spiritual aspirations, a genuine need to discover more, a dissatisfaction with what they were, a frustration with the same week in, week out type of church service that was frankly boring, verging on the pointless and the irrelevant, unconnected with the daily concerns of life.

A man in his early forties, Monay knew his own mind but was not forceful in forwarding an opinion. An appealing openness about his face expressed a frank character that had nothing to hide or be ashamed of. Not wishing to stagnate, nor settle for second best and become a poor parody of what he hoped for, Monay aspired to realise all he could become through the transforming hand of God.

Monay's life had been saved by a sneeze. His parents, already having three young children, decided to follow the tribal tradition of burying alive an unwanted baby, as the family doubted their ability to provide food for another mouth. The newly born, prepared for his macabre funeral, had sneezed, which according to folklore belief, indicated the entering of his spirit into his body. Now considered taboo to proceed with the funeral of a living soul, Monay was spared. Once a teenager, he decided to follow Christ and, recognising that God had had a purpose in saving him during the first hours of life, Monay devoted himself to his Lord. He went to the Bible school up north and after graduating, helped to establish a new church back among the Buhid, across the central mountain divide. He had been in Batangan a number of years before our arrival and was respected as being their spiritual leader.

The meeting went on late. The distant chatter of the neighbouring households finally ceased long after the pots and plates of the evening meal had been cleared away. An older man in our meeting fell sound asleep. No one was in the least perturbed (or thought of giving him a poke) until the decision had been made to pray aloud simultaneously before departing for home. After all had silently gone, we lingered on the balcony of our new home, intrigued by the blinking light from the fireflies in the nearby kamansi tree. These made their way across the river behind the house to where a great number of their kind winked enticingly in remarkable profusion, where the river ran under the dark bank of the jungle.

Ernesto had already settled down for the night on the floor beneath a side window. A short while later, a commotion from Ernesto's corner of the room roused us.

First we heard what sounded like a child landing on the floor from a height, immediately followed by Ernesto's startled cry. A scuffle of feet punctuated the silence. I came through with my torch to find Ernesto peering at me with the squinting eyes of one rudely awakened – and used to wearing glasses. He explained, 'I think a dog jumped in through the window...' Ernesto stopped, instinctively ducking as the alarmed dog alighted on the far end of the dining table bench. The beam of the torch momentarily picked the dog out. Launching itself off the end of the bench, it leapt mid-air above Ernesto's startled head, and out through the open window.

The next morning we opened the large latticed shutters inset with squares of capis shell which, being partly translucent, allowed in a certain light. The grass roof tops of the neighbouring houses running down to the main street greeted us, and beyond rose a steep grassy hill with a flat top across the Batangan River, with higher, tree-clad hills beyond. The air, cool and fresh, was something we had not known during the three years spent in Batangas and Victoria.

'It's like something from a television documentary!' Alexandra remarked, expressing the same incredulity that nearly had me pinching myself to check whether it was all a dream.

After breakfasting on ripe bananas and papaya and a little bread left over from the previous day, Ernesto said his farewells, leaving before the sun was up over the crest of the hill.

A smiling, sturdily built man in his mid-thirties came up onto the balcony. We exchanged pleasantries. After a while he asked, 'Who is going to help you buy the corrugated roofing for the repairs we talked about last night?'

'Apparently someone called Yaba!' I recalled this information from a conversation I had just had with one of the church elders.

My visitor smiled good-naturedly, remarking, 'That's me!' I then vaguely recognised him to be the one, who together with his wife had helped Ligaya (Joy) in perfecting the translation work more than a year before.

Yaba and I took the jeepney out to Roxas (pronounced Rohas), a town an hour away on the coast. The rough dusty roads skirted the hills before joining the metalled surfaced highway that swept us past the paddy fields of the plains to the coast. In Roxas we ordered what was needed at the builder's merchant, then left to collect later. The sun was fierce in this treeless town of asphalt and concrete and I noticed Yaba was as troubled by the heat as I was. He stripped himself of the shirt he had been wearing open, jacket style, and wound this around his head in turban fashion, leaving him still clothed in a vest. He didn't mind the image he had now adopted of a labourer, no longer caring to be presentable in the eyes of townsfolk out of the practical concern of keeping cooler.

I treated Yaba to a bowl of noodles at a market stall. People passing down the sweltering street looked at us twice, curious why an *Amerikano* was eating with a road worker or rice planter? Noodles finished and still having time to kill, we wandered at a gentle pace down the street. Yaba stopped at the window of the electrical goods shop where banks of televisions were all tuned into a basketball game. We stopped a long time. I looked at Yaba, wondering if we were about to move on. The mesmerised look in his eyes told me he was there to stay for a good while yet, enjoying both the game and the novelty of watching television. Remarking I had a few purchases to make in the market, I wandered on, and bought some stock cubes to add flavour to a stew of the sweet potatoes and leaf tops, pumpkin and pulses that had been brought to the house the night before by various visitors in a generous display of welcome.

The jeepney preparing to leave Batangan
Dr Douglas Kennedy

The corrugated roofing was collected later from the builder's merchant and loaded onto the public service jeepney, already well crammed with goods and people. Accommodating the long roof sheets involved having to rearrange everybody else's merchandise of boxes and sawn timber, a sack of cement and feed sacks of 'Hog Starter' and 'Rooster Booster' to enable the corrugated sheets to be laid flat along the length of the roof. I pitched in to lend a hand, feeling apologetic for the inconvenience. No one heaved a sigh or cast an unfriendly glance. This carriage of goods was quite the norm where the masses used public transport not only for themselves but also for transporting bulk purchases that back home would have required hiring a van!

Seated up there, scorching hot with at least twenty others, I perched on a small, neatly arranged pile of hollow cement blocks. I curled a toe under the grab rail round the edge of the roof to provide a bare modicum of safety on this precarious perch that boded ill in an emergency stop. The sweat pores opened in the midday glare and the thermal rise off the concrete streets and corrugated iron rooftops all about. All were very glad when the jeepney rasped out a final series of hoots and the engine revved loudly, bringing the latecomers running from the market. We were on our way at last! At least I thought we were when to my surprise, after having turned a few blocks of Roxas, we pulled up where we had left a couple of minutes earlier!

Sure enough there were more passengers: two fat women – *tinderas* – small store owners, carrying an enormous polythene sack between them, even larger than the fatter of the two, a colourful bag bulging with packets of crisps and biscuits. Off once again and now greatly looking forward to the open road to get some breeze from the cooler air from the paddy fields, I gritted my teeth when a woman's voice from down below told the driver to pull over at a pharmacy stall. Did none of these women have any pity for us poor guys wilting on top of the roof? The woman got out, had an infernally long chat with the owner of the chemist and came back to the jeepney empty-handed. We were off again with the same hopeful thoughts of leaving this sweltering concrete town.

'*Para!*' shouted the same woman's voice as we approached another pharmacy, at which the driver obligingly pulled up. Down from the rear step went the woman, waving a doctor's prescription as she went over to the counter. An attractive girl dressed in a white chemist's coat took the receipt and stared at it a long while. She turned the sheet of paper over to see if anything was written on the back, which there wasn't. She turned it back over again and studied it a long time with a quizzical expression that made her impeccably plucked brows waver.

'Oh, come on,' I wanted to blurt out, 'you've either got it or you haven't!' The girl knitted her brow and continued to examine the prescription intently. Could she read or was she just a beautiful accompaniment for the shop to attract more custom? Finally she handed over the prescription to an older colleague, and set about what she was undoubtedly better skilled at doing, combing her luxuriantly long hair, which she secured in a ponytail with an enormous scarlet scrunchie. After an interminable wait, the prescription was finally brought to an old Chinese-looking woman sitting behind a desk raised up on a platform. The old lady was not dressed in white and judging by her elevated position, she must have been the owner. She looked at it disinterestedly and with a single shake of the head indicated they did not stock that particular medicine. She cast a dismissive glance at the customer; her lacklustre eyes, insensitive to her customer's plight, were the epitome of detachment.

I resigned myself to a few more stops before we could reach the relief of the open road. I could hear snatches of the explanation from the prescription-bearing woman to the occupants in the jeepney below. The medicine was for her sick husband who had 'high blad'. We didn't have far to travel before reaching the next pharmacy and yet two more after that. Roxas was full of chemists! Was this place a retirement centre?

I looked at Yaba to see how he was coping with all these irritating stops. He had now removed the shirt wrapped around his brow and had draped it, open fashion, over his recumbent head. I wished I could have switched off like that!

'My husband's urine is very brown in the mornings,' I heard the prescription woman telling the growing number of passengers who were becoming more curious about her husband's ailments. She was plied with questions in an engaging way, probably helping to keep at bay a sense of irritation over the delay.

Eventually we had done a full circuit of the pharmacies in that quarter of Roxas and pulled up at the store where the prescription bearer had had a lengthy chat with the store-keeper. A purchase was made! Why didn't she buy it in the first place and spare us from the fruitless round? Apparently she had settled for the generic name of the brand listed on the prescription. No wonder her husband had high blood pressure!

The following day, two other Buhid joined Yaba and Monay in repairing the damaged roof. They extended a corrugated sheet section over the back porch where previously the run-off from the roof had fallen directly onto the bamboo flooring, causing it to rot. More importantly they rebuilt the outside toilet which had collapsed in a typhoon. The unharmed toilet bowl had been the prized luxury the Hanselmans had purchased in their latter years. The Buhid said that using sawn timber to rebuild the booth would be costly and take a day or two to get. We suggested bamboo; Ernesto advised against it, remarking that cheeky children would amuse themselves peeping through the cracks! However, we decided to risk the bamboo solution since it was readily available, determining to deal with any cheeky chappie who might snigger at us through the cracks. We need not have worried – Buhid children didn't seem in the slightest bit interested to see if we were the same as them without trousers!

Within the first week, our house and surrounds received much attention. The majority of the congregation had come after the midweek prayer meeting in the morning to re-establish a fence. This was made from freshly cut branches, thrust into the ground in a line at one-inch intervals, and lashed together with lengths of strong vine. We had not requested this to be done. However, the Buhid probably felt it right to mark out our territory as perhaps had been the practice of our predecessors. Soon after, the fence budded and came into leaf, but it was only a matter of a couple of months before adult pigs forced their way through, hopeful of better food on our side. Children further opened the gap in no time at all after that. Sections of stakes that had not budded mysteriously disappeared without trace – I suspect the evidence of smoke from the neighbour's cooking fires perhaps gave the best clue as to why these had disappeared.

Sunday came and the church 'bell' was struck, a short girder of steel suspended from a sturdy branch of a frangipani tree growing some hundred metres from the dilapidated church building. Before everyone congregated in the church building, small groups formed all over the town, the children dividing into different age groups and the adults segregated by gender. This was 'Sanday skul'. Yan-yan – the bright Buhid representative on the Mangyan Church Association – led the youth group and had already asked for my input. A well-to-do Buhid, relatively speaking, Yan-yan had built a second house of sawn timber, with a concrete base and a tin roof right at the 'Kanto'. The Kanto was the most desired piece of real estate in the whole village, the junction of the path coming down from the Christian area of Madling, with the main street. Here folk of all ages gathered after breakfast to see the first jeepney off and congregated again at sunset when the second and last trip of the day brought the high school students back home again together with those who had shopped in the town. The Kanto buzzed with activity at these times of day, making it the place to be in a setting that had no television to provide distraction, entertainment and the news of the day.

Yan-yan's house was most compact; a store room occupied the ground floor, and the upstairs, designed as the living quarters, could welcome guests as well as providing a place which the youth group appreciated. The small, rectangular room snugly accommodated us all, as we huddled shoulder to shoulder lining the four walls, squeezing about twenty of us into a space westerners would have found cramped for five.

Johnny, the most mature-looking lad, played the guitar quite ably, although it took him a good while to warm up at the start of each song, experimenting through a range of chords to determine in which key to set the songs. Singing shyly at first, but overcoming their initial reserve, they sang with gusto and sometimes with feeling. They clearly enjoyed worshipping and needed no coercing. This 20-minute singing was followed by a Bible study Yan-yan led, making various ones read Bible verses before named individuals were asked questions. The high school students had little difficulty in answering; not that they were always correct, but they felt no inhibition. But others, who had perhaps only completed two or three years at primary school before taking up farming full-time, were shy to answer, embarrassed that they probably didn't know the right answer. One or two illiterate ones struggled with this part of the activity, not that they necessarily had inferior intellectual ability, but were often handicapped in thinking that this was the case. Parents in Batangan tended to send their children to the primary school across on the other side of town, usually doing two to three years of schooling. Just the brighter ones continued, graduating onto high school, but only if the family could afford to fund their books, uniform and jeepney fare. Not all who had the potential to succeed at high school had the means to go.

Occasionally the one who had the financial means lacked the ability. The youngest of many siblings, Bernabe had high hopes pinned upon him. He was the first child whom the parents were able to fund through high school. 'Maybe one day Bernabe will be a doctor,' his ageing mother wistfully said, punctuating the remark with a warm-hearted laugh. She covered her mouth with her hand, a habit in the Philippines which often conveyed embarrassment. Did she really think therefore that her hope was preposterous? If so, why did she frequently state this wish?

Poor Bernabe would be sent round to our house with his English homework many an evening after school. The lad was reluctant but Daginay – his ambitious mother – could be heard prompting him from the night shadows in a stage whisper somewhere about where our fence used to stand.

'Go on, Bernabe – ask them to help you, they won't mind!'

Bernabe did not move at the first or the second summons, but stood there indecisively, ruffling his ample hair in his consternation. By the fourth or fifth time, Daginay's tone had noticeably changed from a whisper to a rasp, 'Bernabe – go! Go now before I take a stick to you!'

And so Bernabe reluctantly drifted over to the front steps of our house and made the most subdued cough imaginable – the Buhid equivalent of ringing a door bell. He hoped his arrival would not be heard and allow him to beat a hasty retreat and tell his mother that the foreigners were out! Trying to coerce Bernabe into answering the questions from his homework was quite hopeless. However creative one was in rephrasing the questions, patiently translating the English and explaining the requirement, Bernabe would look blankly at his book and not move a limb. He was either hopelessly shy or completely dense. We wrote down the required answers eventually, hoping that the mere copying of these into his jotter might help the development of his English. The only time Bernabe smiled was when we released him from these tortuous sessions with the foreigners.

'This is our *faduwasay* Martin and *faduwasay* Alexandra,' Yan-yan introduced us to the youth group, who for the first time momentarily met our gaze. 'They are in the school holidays now,' Yan-yan continued, turning now to us, 'and perhaps you wouldn't mind if they wanted to come round to your house?'

'We would be delighted,' Alexandra replied with her radiant smile.

'Maybe you would all like to come round as a group one night,' I ventured. Encouraged by the bright faces of a couple of the girls, I added, 'Why not come tomorrow night and we'll sing some worship songs on the balcony, study a little from the Bible and play some games!'

Yan-yan was clearly delighted with the suggestion and in order to firm up the invitation asked when they should come tomorrow night.

'At about half past six,' I replied.

Yan-yan smiled patiently. 'Let's say just at first dark would be about the right time!'

A tribal church is a noisy one, continuously restless, with babies screaming, children shouting and running about, and dogs, pigs and chickens coming and going – even snakes entering on a couple of occasions. When I think of the reaction a snake would make on entering a church back home, the sangfroid of the Buhid truly amazed me as they quietly dispatched them with little fuss and the preacher did not even pause in his sermon.

The leading of the service was a very communal event, with no one dominating, and varied from week to week, each bringing their own slant and personality through what they shared. The congregation had a laid-back manner, some men leaning against their wives, others picking out nits from the hair of the one in front. No one dressed smartly for the occasion. The entire morning was given over to attending to these two things: Sunday school and church.

After a hot siesta under our tin roof, we walked up the Batangan River from the busy village of probably 150 grass-roofed huts till we reached the school at the far end and the jungle beyond. A troupe of children trailed us and kept growing. Just beyond the school, the river ran three inches above the knee and here we chose to bathe. We bathed in our shorts and the girls kept their T-shirts on. The water was tepid, cool at first on sweaty skin but wonderful once submerged and of a temperature in which you could remain all day. These bath times provided the main occasion to chat and chill out. But on this occasion, it was not relaxing.

Forty-seven children had assembled and silently lined the banks, staring like statues at these white foreign bodies in their river, fascinated particularly by my hirsute form. The following day their number had reduced to 29, then 18 the day after. Thankfully, our novelty value eventually wore off and we learned to take more discreet ways to less populated spots further into the jungle.

Iain and Hannah named a couple of these favoured spots. The closer of the two became known as the 'Cool Pool' at the foot of a tiny waterfall with a large flat slab of rock ideal for laying out your toiletries and laundry on. The other pool was further and in rainy season could be guaranteed to be foamy and forceful, opening into a largish basin that could accommodate the entire family at once (unlike the Cool Pool where we had to take turns). For a reason even unknown to our children, this large pool was named 'The Spoon of Lagoon'. This powerful waterfall poured over a sloping, smooth slab of rock that you could slide down like on a shoot, propelling you with force into the foaming pool below. We tumbled in the depths for at least a single somersault in the force of the current, but the commotion was short-lived as the river calmed just beyond the fall. By allowing ourselves to drift, eventually we would be washed up on the stony island downstream, excellent for scouring the skin with its fine shingle, leaving the body feeling tingly clean. We later discovered that the Spoon of Lagoon provided the church's baptistery, ideal in depth for immersing fully-grown adults. It amused us that the church members said of their missionaries that they bathed in the baptistery! In dry season, when the water was low, the congregation built a rock dam just downstream of the basin, lined with banana leaves to make it more watertight.

On the Monday night, a couple of sixteen-year-old girls tentatively came onto our balcony just at nightfall, smiling shyly all the while.

'Are we meeting here now?' they managed to ask us after a while. Hearing our assent they looked at one another and both simultaneously did a little jump before turning towards the steps. The last one looked back and explained, 'We'll just go and get the others!'

The others couldn't have been far away, probably lurking in the shadow of a home or under a tree, for within a minute, the balcony was swamped with young people, not only filling the bench seats but sitting on the floor. I climbed on top of the wooden balustrade of the balcony to hang the pressure lantern from a roof beam; its white shield, fixed just above the glass, reflected the light effectively onto the throng of expectant faces. The bright illumination penetrated deep into the darkness, sending shafts of light between huts and trees, far across the river.

Their excitement was of the kind of being truly thrilled – overawed by the sense of occasion, similar to the way I remember feeling when I went to see my first rock band in a live concert! Such heightened expectation we feared would result in profound disappointment, considering the ordinariness of the programme we had arranged. We sang some worship songs accompanied by guitar, followed by a Bible study and quiz and ended introducing them to Mikado – or Pick-up Sticks as it is sometimes called. They played with serious intent and with such a light touch, crouching silently around the hardboard sheet we had placed over the bamboo floor slats, moving stealthily on the sticks as though stalking a bird, intent on taking it by surprise. All felt the tension together, until another stick was accidentally moved and they could express the relief with shouts of laughter. They struck me as being a very homogenous whole, jointly engaging and feeling emotion corporately.

These balcony meetings became regular events, always well attended although the initial wonder did wane somewhat; nevertheless it did not curb their enthusiasm. They enjoyed dramatising Bible stories. The first one performed was the raising of Lazarus. We let them decide who was going to play which part.

'So who is going to play the part of Lazarus?' I opened the bidding. Johnny's hand shot up enthusiastically. Almost immediately he withdrew it again, surprised by his own audacity; he seemed genuinely taken aback by his own forwardness. Johnny was nominated for the part. He assumed this would be the leading role and we admit to being quietly amused on observing the vague sense of disappointment which came over his face when he discovered he was to die in act one and only be raised to life again right at the end of the play!

Johnny was determined to make the most of his small part, and died in a very operatic way. He moaned, 'A'ray – a'ray!' waving an arm pathetically, and looking imploringly at the two girls who were playing his sisters. Everyone was relieved when he did eventually give up the ghost, slumping back heavily upon the bench. He had to lie still, but peeped out of the corner of his eye at his sisters.

'Cry louder!' Lazarus whispered.

The sisters laughed and couldn't control themselves for a while.

'You love me,' continued Lazarus, 'so you are really upset that I have died!' The dead man directed from under his shroud whilst being carried away to his tomb. 'Weep louder for me – I am your beloved brother!' This resulted in quite the contrary effect to what he earnestly felt appropriate.

Amusing as these rehearsals were, they in no way matched the hilarity on the day of the production when acted for real and Johnny kept up these stage directions after he had supposedly uttered his last 'A'ray!' Johnny had now thought it an integral part of the act to direct his own funeral. The acting was greatly appreciated and Johnny did indeed emerge with a sense of real triumph from the dead when his moment of glory did finally come. Unable to conceal his pleasure and forgetting to be just as surprised as his sisters to have come alive again, he cajoled them once more before the whole church:

All shiny chrome transport
Dr Douglas Kennedy

'Look happy now, I am alive again!' He mimed with his hands for them to throw their arms in the air as he dramatically discarded the shroud.

The youth group went on to perform a memorable Christmas drama the following year. Played at night on Christmas Eve, the sudden and alarming appearance of an angel was put to good effect by one unexpectedly emerging to perch on various windowsills of the poorly lit church, draped in white sheeting and holding a dazzlingly bright pressure lantern. As Monay's son, playing the part of the angel Gabriel, climbed up into the window alcove from outside, his sheet came loose. With one hand already holding the window frame for support, he grabbed hold of his falling robe with the other which was also holding the furiously hot lantern.

We watched the folds of the sheet about him smouldering against the Pyrex glass of the lantern and a mysterious arm or two appeared from outside the window to prevent Gabriel going up in flames. The angel maintained his composure all the while, dramatically delivering his tidings.

Chapter Seven:

The Pied Piper *Aswang*

Hagan stopped by the wayside, drew out his *fotol* from its hand-carved sheath and, taking hold of a straight branch, lopped it off. He set to work immediately, cleaning the limb with the ease of one used to handling a machete daily, fashioning it into a walking staff. Testingly he lent his weight on it, before setting off at rapid pace down the mountainside. Well into his sixties, grey-haired but still strong in body, Hagan was so fast that he gradually put more and more distance between us as we set off down the mountain trail in his tracks. Three other Buhid companions walked with us over to Siyangi, and with the exception of Monay, who had his young daughter in tow, the others were in hot pursuit of the grandfather of the group. Once those 20 and 30 years his junior were hot upon his heels, Hagan put his staff to maximum effect as a third leg, propelling his body, more guided than supported, through the air. The older man, maintaining his supremacy, whooped with delight as he careered down the hillside, barely touching the ground, skimming the dust like a flat pebble skims the surface of the water. The younger men whooped with delight too to see his splendid deer-like leaps that left them with no hope of keeping up.

The difficulty of the climb out of the Batangan river valley was more due to heat than it being particularly steep. The tropical humidity made a climb in easy terrain and of no great distance into a challenge. Beyond the hill ridge, a light grey gravel and boulder-strewn river course marked the progress of the Siyangi River through the forest-clad hills. What looked like jungle in the distance to the untrained eye were cultivated hillsides of banana and citrus trees, coconut palms and bamboo. To be out in the hills, especially with the energy and light-heartedness of the Buhid as companions who pointed things out that the outsider invariably missed, was a joy and a wonder.

An inscription carved onto the living stem of bamboo was drawn to my attention, written in the ancient script of Malay origin that only survives today on Mindoro among the Buhid and Hanunoo Mangyan. With the point of a *fotol* or a sharpened stylus of a bamboo twig, a cut is made through the thin green membrane of the stem. This inscription was written by one lamenting over his field, which by day was being eaten by rats and by night was ploughed up by wild pigs, using their snouts in search of yams.

'We have other poems too!' remarked Monay, 'ones written by a boy to a girl he admires. Maybe he will carve his poem on a wayside bamboo on the trail his love takes to her father's field so that she might notice and better still, write her reply upon it!'

'What other ways can a lad show that he likes a girl?' I asked.

'By collecting firewood for her father,' Umyagan laughed. 'A young man is eager to prove he is able to care and provide for a girl. He will fetch water as well!'

'I had to fetch loads of water and firewood before my wife and her family noticed me and took me seriously!' remarked Hagan.

The water flowing in the Siyangi River was cool, soothing scorched skin, reviving strength and encouraging fresh determination to complete the trail.

I entered into something of the euphoria a water buffalo must feel when sinking down into cool waters after a hot, gruelling walk. The remainder of the way criss-crossed the gravel scree of the flood valley, a way shown by the stones smoothed by the tramp of many feet along the shingle bed. The way was hot in this treeless gravel wilderness where the strong sunlight relentlessly glared off the bleached boulders, making eyes squint and partially colour-blind under the intensity of the light. The shade of the bamboo and coconuts growing about the village of Siyangi was a relief to reach. On a flat, grassy place beside a low cliff top, stood the thirty-five houses, those nearest the river abandoned as each flood ate away more from the pebble conglomerate cliff. Along the cliff top, the village had a sad air about it.

Not presuming upon anyone's hospitality, our small party sat upon some boulders under the shade of a spreading tree. Word soon spread that Hagan and Monay and others, including the new missionary, had arrived from Batangan. Led to Paladan's house, we answered some inquiries, and dozed whilst supper was being prepared, resting weary limbs stretched out on a bamboo floor that could feel hard and unyielding, but on this occasion had a vague elasticity to it. The less weary chatted away sporadically, exchanging village news. It was only after the supper of rice and the nuts and flesh of the kamansi boiled in coconut juice had been eaten that the conversation grew more animated, when neighbours drifted in with the usual questions to establish my identity. Talking incessantly all evening I was relieved to unravel my blanket at what felt like a very late hour and place this down alongside ten or more others in the inner room. Most Buhid houses have an inner room, the outer one being like a reception-cum-corridor close to the kitchen and leading into the inner

Our 'kitchen' in Siyangi
Martin Haworth

sanctum of the sleeping area. In Paladan's house, the sleeping quarters were accessed by a two-and-a-half foot step up onto a higher bamboo platform.

The next conscious moment was not morning (which otherwise it would have been given a softer bed than the bamboo floor slats), but sometime in the dead of night. At various stages, I woke with an arm or a leg having gone dead (often both), necessitating a change of posture. After a few nights of sleeping as the Mangyan sleep, the body automatically shifts position periodically through the night without being roused to a state of disconsolate consciousness.

The uncertain dawn light peeped in pale and ghost-like through the cracks of the woven bamboo walls. Someone began to pray aloud, lying just where he was, loath to leave the blanket warmth. Instantaneously, everyone else in the room began to pray aloud, a few with fervour, others sleepily, some opening with the words, 'Good morning, Lord!' Only after everyone had first prayed did anyone start a conversation. As the bedding was folded up and clothes that had been used for pillows packed away, I noticed that the light had already intensified through the wall cracks, now bright, almost shaft-like, dispersing the gloom of our sleeping quarters.

That first trip had only been brief, time to be introduced at the Sunday worship meeting, with an opportunity for me to teach. The next visit was with Alexandra, 16 months later. We had been back in Scotland as a family for a year on what was known as 'Home Assignment' – a time to renew links with our sending church and other supporting churches. On returning to the Philippines, a routine medical check-up required by immigration law, revealed me to be suffering from TB, delaying our getting back to the villages.

Once my strength began to return after the effects of the strong TB drugs, we made arrangements to be met at the Lisap bridge by the folk from Siyangi. We were their visitors from the start rather than being considered among the company from Batangan. Accompanied from Lisap by Imyan bringing her husband Anaw back from Calapan, we made slow time. Anaw had had an appendectomy just two days beforehand and was still understandably sore from the operation. We felt for him, conveyed back to the village in an ambulance that was a *kariton* – a bullock cart with two solid wooden wheels drawn by a water buffalo. Although the buffalo went at a helpfully slow pace, the way was so uneven that the *kariton* lurched this way and that, every bump registering in the pained expression of the invalid. It was desperately hot at midday in this stony wilderness.

The Buhid children especially enjoyed our arrival, the first foreigners that many of them had ever seen. The older ones could well remember the Hanselmans and so news of our arrival did not have quite the same effect on them. Recalling how not to presume on anyone's hospitality, we let Anaw and Imyan proceed on to their house whilst we lingered outside the church. Imyan turned back and came for us even before removing her husband from the *kariton*.

'Don't wait around there,' she almost chided us, 'there's a house you can sleep in next to our own!' We took up our backpacks and followed her through the muddy gap between two houses. Anaw was now sitting on the edge of the floor of his home – a home he had grown to especially cherish. When he had heard of the grave need for an operation, he wondered if he would ever make it home again. No wonder he sat there grinning so much.

Shown to a tiny hut to the side of their far more substantial house, we eyed with appreciation the simple rectangular home with two doors at the front. One door led into the main room; the other led to a lower level, a tiny corridor, an under-the-stairs cupboard in dimensions, containing some half-filled sacks. There a person could lie down only if he were to curl up. In the main room we could lie full stretch and it felt substantial in comparison, although my head and feet touched the opposite walls! Indeed miniature, it was rather like living in a fine tree house.

One of the houses provided for the Hanselmans was so small that the tall Roberto had to sleep at night with his feet dangling out of the front door! For once I was thankful for being on the small side for a westerner. Always wishing she were taller, Alexandra once bumped her head on a Filipino door lintel, a first-of-its-kind event she announced with a note of triumph!

That night we gathered in the church to be introduced, for none of them had met Alexandra before. A pressure lantern we had brought sent a surprisingly bright light through all the church and beyond. The flood of bright, smiling faces in front of us, coupled with the adulation of the children, was quite overwhelming for quite a private kind of couple like us. The church building was not big enough to contain all, for children came with parents, teenagers gathered in one corner, older folk took up position near the front, whilst the back row was crowded with young dads with mischievous grins. We had also brought a guitar, compliments of the Sunday school of our home church. The £100 gift had enabled us to buy four guitars and a year's set of Sunday school lessons for each of the four main Buhid churches!

But no one knew how to play the guitar. In such circumstances, I can be persuaded to play. With such a hugely appreciative congregation, I could have become big-headed if I entertained any aspirations of becoming an accomplished guitar player. Unfortunately, I can only play when following written chords, whereas the Buhid (true of all Filipinos we met) have the ability to anticipate all the chord changes correctly and instinctively. But no such person was here in the Siyangi Church. I only knew how to play Tagalog songs and none of the Buhid ones yet, as I had not transcribed the chords into the Buhid hymnal.

Leading with songs they had heard on the early morning Christian radio broadcast from Manila, the worship was lively if not accurate. We felt uncomfortable with these imported worship songs, especially since they had very good ones of their own, but the Buhid assured us these were quite appropriate.

'Don't you know that God can understand Tagalog as well?' challenged one short woman, silencing our expressed misgivings.

The following morning brought the request to write out all the words to the Tagalog choruses. Then their main elder, Buhadan, appearing with a cassette recorder, asked me to play and to sing through the entire repertoire. Painful as it was for me to hear the recordings replayed, they nevertheless loved it and sang along to the tape. Two or three of them wanted to learn the guitar and free time passed teaching these beginners in the only way I knew, by the very western approach of drawing diagrams of finger positions on the frets. They found interpreting the chord charts extremely difficult, unable for quite a while to grasp such representation.

All that week the children followed us, making us feel like the Pied Piper of Hamden with an entire retinue shadowing us down to the river for our mid-afternoon bathe. They followed us in a gaggle to the spring to draw water, and gathered around with great fascination to watch me ignite the pressure lantern at night. We had to be cunning to give them the slip when we wanted to go to relieve ourselves in the woods! Not only the children, but their parents too, sought us out with childlike glee, bringing gifts of food, taking the opportunity to reminisce at length about Roberto and Ligaya.

Living in Siyangi was far more basic than the life we had now grown accustomed to in Batangan. Batangan had the luxury of an outside toilet, a paraffin stove, not

Our presence amuses
Dr Douglas Kennedy

to mention a house in which we could stand up and walk about – and even sit on a chair at the mahogany slab table.

We cooked the main meal on an open wood fire outside the house, under an extended grass and bamboo eave section of Anaw's house. Three stones stood on end provided a tripod-like base for our cooking pot to rest upon; one pot for rice, the other for a vegetable stew. Neighbours kept us well supplied with dry, easily combustible wood. Tree resin gathered in a leaf cone, left to harden, provided a highly effective firelighter. Breaking off a piece no larger than the end of your thumb, the resin would ignite on contact with the flame from a match and would burn effectively for five minutes, time enough for the wood to catch. Care had to be taken to avoid the burning resin dripping like wax onto the skin as it burned with intensity.

These resin leaf cones are also used in some houses for light by clamping it in a tripod-shaped branch, placed on the floor. The resin burns with a bitter sweet aromatic smell which I found most evocative of Mindoro nights spent in the hills, oddly an aroma that most Buhid do not find so pleasant.

With lengthy cooking times, we ate just the one main meal at lunchtime, feeding on leftovers for supper supplemented with ripe bananas and other fruit given to us. Passion fruit grew prolifically here on a vine which we regarded as a great treat. Pigs are very fond of passion fruit too and we were thankful they couldn't climb.

Many other daily chores kept us busy, like fetching water; this entailed a convenient five-minute walk to where a fresh supply of spring water was conveyed along a bamboo conduit raised on stilts. Laundering down in the river using an effective soap that lathered well in cold water, was a therapeutic occupation – provided the chore was done daily and not left to accumulate into a large pile. This also reduced the number of clothes needed to be brought to just the three sets including what we were wearing, enabling us to travel lighter. Since laundering was done in conjunction with our daily bathe, it just became a natural extension to washing ourselves.

The remainder of the day was spent visiting, being visited and teaching guitar. Last minute revision of materials for the twice-daily teaching and worship sessions, or sometimes even for a third session, had to be squeezed in too. Many were off to their fields during the daytime, but the sick were prayed for, treated in whatever way we could, and the elderly were encouraged. Busily weaving a basket or a skirt, mothers became less shy with us and aired their concerns. The skirts were woven on looms tensioned by the weaver wearing a belt attachment to the loom and kept taut by her pushing her feet against the house wall. Some of the men would sometimes be at home during one of the slack periods in the agricultural cycle. There was always plenty to do: wood to collect, a water buffalo to wash down in the river, pigs to feed, food to gather for the next meal. So when not pushed to prepare their land, the Buhid tended to go about these lighter tasks a little later in the day than usual or aimed to finish early in the afternoon by starting promptly in the morning.

Occasionally we joined Buhid in their food gathering, if their fields were not too far. Rudling, our neighbour, used to have a craving for shrimps from time to time and I would join him to grope about in the water, turning over stones to catch a glimpse of one of these reclusive creatures. He made a pair of goggles out of wood shaped to fit round his eye sockets utilising the glass from the base of a soft drinks bottle for the lens, carefully and patiently filed down to fit into the wooden goggle holders. He had fashioned them expertly into just the right shape, making them watertight with the application of some hot resin dripped into the join to form a seal. The rubber strap that went round the back of his head was the only purchased piece; a durable band normally used for making catapults.

The spear gun was equally ingenious. Fashioned out of a single piece of wood, the gun was carved with a *fotol* into a pistol shape. This too had an elastic strip fixed to a launch pin that fired a skewer-like bolt from the gun. The skewer only had a three-inch travelling distance before it came to an abrupt halt, so the user had to be up close and have split second reactions when hoping to spear a shrimp.

Largely self-sufficient, the Buhid had acquired a liking for rice which needed to be bought. Rice crops do not yield plentifully when sown in a dry field, dependent upon the seasonal rains, as opposed to the ideal conditions of a submerged paddy. This was a telling sign of the Buhid moving on from their forest gathering traditions only within the last generation or two, and becoming agriculturists. Their mountain produce had to be traded in order to buy rice. But those who didn't aspire to eating rice daily could adequately live on the various root crops such as yams and of course cooking bananas – a diet they rightly profess to be 'very dull'!

On our first visit to Siyangi, many attended church; particularly young couples, numerous at that time. Some were in the habit of coming on a Sunday morning, whilst others had given up coming at all, preferring to play basketball or visit the market at Lisap instead. Drawn by curiosity, they wondered what these strangers had to share; our foreignness intrigued as most were too young to remember hearing the Hanselmans' teaching. But they had mixed motives too; we were considered a source of amusement as we spoke their language poorly and conversed in the national language sometimes quaintly to their ears, providing an entertainment to a people who had no television. A few may have been there who truly had spiritual concerns, though.

All the young men congregated on the back row, where there was much joking and a sense of camaraderie, set apart from their wives who sat up near the front tending to their youngest children at the breast. As the days progressed, they discovered God's Word was relevant, speaking to their fear of evil spirits, inspiring faith through the daily uncertainties of life, and showing them the need to trust God. Identifying God as all-loving and all-powerful, able to heal people without doctors and medicine, a Lord of order who spoke to the individual about sorting out marital problems as well as speaking to the nations about matters of justice, was largely new to them. Those who came to jest and scoff came under the powerful effect of God, not just through his Word but by his Spirit. God had a purpose and a concern for these Buhid lives that was not lost on them. It confirmed to us how worthwhile all those years of preparation had been, waiting for such a time as this to feed spiritually hungry people. Because of a strong faith that suddenly came into evidence, their prayers were answered, many concerning health matters.

As many came into a relationship with God, they became keen to learn. One effective way of understanding biblical narrative was to dramatise it, allowing their imagination to enter into the experience of the characters and events. In this way the spiritual principles were not lost, but had a practical framework familiar and pertinent to their own situation. The dramas were enjoyed by all, old and young, believer and those generally indifferent to the Christian message, filling the church with a happy and expectant throng, waiting to see their child or an aunt perform their part. Dramas were often followed up with a quiz, the correct answers plotting a team's progress on the chalkboard by colouring in another stage of a biblical journey on a ready drawn map. Church took on a whole new meaning to them.

From spiritual indifference, suddenly a great number wanted to learn for themselves not just when we were present, but between our quarterly visits, causing a great demand for Bibles from those able to read adequately and for Scripture comics from the semi-literate. Wherever we went, we were now accompanied by several boxes filled with books and medicine.

Equipped with Bibles, those over forty years old had difficulties reading the small print. With the cost of reading glasses beyond their means, we made one appeal in a prayer letter to send us unwanted spectacles and soon a steady supply came in shoeboxes.

One church elder had had a pair of glasses since the Hanselmans' time and with his sight obviously deteriorating, he had to wear the lenses at a 45 degree angle to his eyes causing the spectacle arms to point up slightly from above his head. Only then could he read by holding the Bible out at arm's length and by raising his chin high in the air. One of the spectacle arms having snapped off had been repaired by binding an old toothbrush on with cotton thread. The sight was made more comical by the small horns that decorated the upper sides of the frame, much in the style some ageing Hollywood actress might have worn in the late fifties! But the elder in question was just thankful to find a replacement pair that enabled him to read clearly again; his gain though meant our loss in no longer being amused every time he read from the front of the church.

Another elderly chap, trying on various pairs of glasses laid out on sheets of newspaper on the floor of our hut, was having no satisfaction whatsoever. Alexandra took a photograph of him just as he placed yet another pair on his nose with the idea of posting this picture to the spectacle donors in Scotland. At the moment the flash went, the old fellow declared with great excitement, 'This is the pair!' due to the instant illumination when placing them on.

The Siyangi Church became vocal about what was largely a new-found faith to most of them, keen to pass on to family and friends something they had discovered to be very meaningful. Having heard about a film in Tagalog on the life of Jesus, they asked if it would be possible to get hold of a copy. Having the promise of film and equipment, a conference date was set to screen the film.

The crew bringing the film equipment from Calapan did not arrive the first night of the conference. Invited friends and family from all the neighbouring villages were understandably disappointed. To make matters worse, one of those torrential tropical downpours persisted for hours, and those unable to find a space within the crammed church were soaked even though they pressed themselves against the windows seeking shelter under the eaves. Such a press of bodies at every opening to the church, obstructing any natural ventilation, made it stifling hot for those within. Everyone was soon aglow, and not just with anticipation.

Diokno, the elder from a large Buhid church at Apnagan, tried to make an address, but without the aid of amplification his voice was hopelessly drowned in the cacophony of torrential rain drumming on the tin roof. Even singing was quite impossible as you couldn't keep time, unable to hear anyone else. An extremely sullen crowd went to bed that night, taking what shelter they could, cramming body to body on all available floor space in every hut. Fearing these unbelievers would head back home the next morning, I promised to go to Calapan at the crack of dawn in search of the film crew.

I left in the half light and the falling rain with Buhadan, a short man of my age, for the bridge two hours away, briskly walking alongside the rising river, now a churning chocolate colour. Leaving Buhadan posted at the Lisap bridge in case the film crew arrived, I made the eight-hour round trip by bus, to discover at Calapan that the film crew had left early that morning. Returning to the Lisap bridge late in the afternoon, Buhadan was still waiting, not having seen the film crew. We walked disconsolately back to Siyangi to find the film crew had arrived half an hour ahead of us! They had taken an unusual route and had stopped off at someone's house for the best part of the day!

At least the equipment worked and the rain held off this second night. I left a mesmerised audience watching the film and went to bed exhausted, wondering what a good many of them made of the film. The majority, who came from the interior, had never seen a film before. They had heard mention of this Jesus and now they were seeing him for the first time, projected by a bright light as a kind of spirit, appearing with many other spirits, moving across a large white sheet suspended along the front of the church. Two and a half hours later, Jesus was gone – his appearance an enigma, and his sudden disappearance equally baffling to them. Christ's presence was somehow connected with a sturdy, black box that projected light and yet another box that chugged quietly away. It was indeed mysterious magic they must have thought the white one with the beard had something to do with. As for those in Siyangi, living closer to the lowlands and having commerce with the Luktanon, such things were no longer a mystery but nevertheless a rare delight.

Communion was celebrated on the Sunday; this found its own expression there in the hills. A large green branch was proffered from the aisle by an officiating elder, from which leaves were broken off and folded into a cone to receive the communion 'wine' in the form of coconut juice. The bread was now usually broken cracker, but in bygone days was more commonly cooked sweet potato or rice. Before the leaves were discarded after communion they were collected and counted – an obvious preoccupation of a western missionary wanting to record the number of communicants, something I cannot imagine any Mangyan being naturally concerned about.

My first communion taken with the Mangyan, was one Easter several years previously at another such conference, where unfortunately I was the cause of changing the solemn mood of remembering the Lord's death. My Mangyan neighbour had shown me how to form the cone out of a leaf. Amazed at this simple art, approving of this no-washing-up cup, I playfully unfolded the leaf and reformed it several times, keen to practise the skill so that next time I would not have to be shown.

The coconut came, my cone was filled, but unlike all the cones about me, mine began to drip steadily. Instructed to hold onto the elements until everyone had been served, before eating and drinking, my cup was quite empty before the appointed moment to drink. My neighbour who had begun to shake with silent laughter whilst watching my emptying cup, stood up and motioned to the elder with the coconut to come back to replenish my cup. Just to ensure it would not happen again, the neighbour carefully folded my leaf and made me take it from him, carefully rearranging my fingers appropriately as a father would teach his child.

As hard as I tried, the leaf cone was steadily dripping again, probably due to being slightly damaged by my refolding it several times earlier. Earnestly trying to preserve a few drops within my leaf, I intently observed the cone, gripping it ever so tightly, trying to ignore my neighbour who was shaking with so much inner laughter I wondered how much longer he could contain himself.

All of a sudden, unobserved from under the benches, a dog came and with one clean and totally unexpected snap, took the piece of cracker carelessly but tantalisingly being dangled from my other hand.

That was it. My neighbour, no longer able to contain himself with the violent heaving silently shaking his entire body, broke out into a sudden but very brief peal of laughter in the midst of the sombre gathering. Throwing his head back, he clutched at his shaking sides. Folk looked round rather disapprovingly at this man who, red in the face, once again checked his hearty laughter. They were more surprised that we, the new missionaries, were at the centre of this quite inappropriate mirth. Word soon got round after communion about the cause of the mirth, with the many people who were shooting telling glances in our direction now amused at what had happened.

By Monday morning, the Siyangi conference was over, with everyone going their separate ways. Buhadan accompanied me on the laborious trail along the alluvial valley to the bridge at Lisap to board the Bongabong jeepney. Tall by Filipino standards and having a full red beard and white skin, I have been often likened to an *aswang* – a spirit being reputedly hairy with untanned skin owing to normally going abroad at night. Parents have often pointed me out, warning their children not to wander off otherwise this *aswang* would get them. Consequently, many Filipino children have initially been frightened of me.

Walking past some Luktanon homes, a jeering remark was shouted: 'Look at the *aswang* walking along with his *duwende*!' *Duwende* were dwarf-like spirits; obviously a reference to the diminutive Buhadan.

Chapter Eight:

Medicine in the Hills

Looking up from attending the fire upon which the rice pot was not boiling, I saw the lower half of a woman tread sure-footedly down the wet, hard-packed clay slope leading to our hut in Apnagan. Her identity was still a mystery for the roof over the kitchen obscured her top half from view. It was raining hard and had been, on and off, the whole week we had been there. Her toes curled up to gain better anchorage on this treacherous slope and I noticed how muddied her calves were, mingled with a small stream of blood where a leech had bitten.

'*Faduwasay!*' the woman greeted me with a note of uneasiness in her voice. (*Faduwasay* was my preferred title simply meaning 'brother' in preference to their previous insistence in using the respectful, but elevated Tagalog title of *Kuya* – 'big brother'.) Inisa smiled coyly, slightly ruffled at finding me and not Alexandra at the cooking fire. She stood outside the porch under a large banana frond she held just above her head. The length of it tapered down her back providing some shelter from the pouring rain.

'Come on in out of the rain,' I urged her, making room for Inisa in our open-sided porch – consisting of just a roof raised over the cooking hearth, with a screen facing the direction of the prevailing wind. 'Where have you come from?'

'Home!' She paused nervously fingering her neck, swollen with a goitre. 'Is Xandra here?'

I called her from within the house. The two women exchanged pleasantries and I concentrated on encouraging the fire to blaze by fanning it with the torn-off side of a cardboard box.

'Do you have any of that iodised salt left?' our visitor asked.

'Yes, I have put a large kilo bag aside for you,' answered Alexandra.

'Oh, I thought it would have all been sold by now. I didn't have the money last week, but we managed to sell some bananas earlier today.'

'I wouldn't have sold your packet,' assured Alexandra. 'You are the one who is most in need of iodised salt – it should prevent your goitre from getting any larger and it will hopefully reduce in size over a period of time if you always use some in your cooking.'

Quite a number of Buhid, almost all of them female, suffered from goitres owing to an iodine deficiency in their diet. Luktanon women did not seem to suffer so much from this problem, probably due to their regularly eating sea fish, a rare treat for those confined to the hills. Moreover, iodised salt was not easy to come by in southern Mindoro and we often had to buy it when visiting the provincial capital and bring some 20 kilos down to our base house, carrying ten kilos to each village, where it quickly sold. Although increasing the weight of our belongings, we had resigned ourselves to no longer travelling light; for besides the salt, there were a further two to three boxes of medicines and Christian literature. The Buhid always carried these up to the hills for us. But sometimes loading it all onto a tricycle to get to the bus was quite a kafuffle and then having to load the several boxes onto a crowded bus, and later off-load onto a tricycle again at the other end was indeed wearisome.

Inisa lingered, in no hurry to get home. Evidently something was on her mind, and she did not delay simply because of the heavy rain, since she was fairly soaked, in spite of the banana leaf. We managed to get her to sit down after the third invitation and asked after the health of her husband, Dalinaw, and each of her children. Beginning to feel a little more relaxed she struck us as being haunted by something. A type of goitre does give the eyes a bulging appearance and although Inisa suffered with this type, the fearful expression in her eyes spoke of one deeply perturbed. After talking around a number of subjects, she suddenly announced, '*Faduwasay* – I'm scared!'

She paused. We waited, giving her time to articulate her feelings.

'The other night, I woke up in the middle of the night aware that something had moved close up to me, just on the other side of the mosquito net. I knew it wasn't one of my children; for although I was very sleepy, not properly awake, I was awake enough to realise it was something strange. Whatever it was didn't move like a person nor was it the size of a human!' She stopped and bit her lower lip. She looked at us both in turn with those eyes standing more prominent than ever. Her nostrils flared as she breathed heavily through her nose and she reminded me of a racehorse, handsome, full of strength, but flighty, champing at the bit.

'It was a huge snake!' she uttered with a shudder of repulsion. 'I woke up Dalinaw and told him a huge snake had just curled up to rest close to my head, just that far away on the other side of the net.' She indicated a couple of feet with her hands. 'Dalinaw had his *fotol* close to hand and crept round the net and killed the thing. I was so scared. The next day, the children and I cleaned up the whole area about our house, cutting down the grass and trimming the branches. There are so many snakes in our parts and more of them are seen in the village these days than ever before.

'That's not all,' Inisia continued, hardly pausing to catch her breath, 'we hear *aswangs* flying about, more than you ever heard before. I'm really frightened… I fear something bad is going to happen soon!'

Aswangs are ferocious spirit beings said to be half-man, half-bird that fly about from dusk onwards, their bite being lethal to humans. Their raucous, crow-like call inspires so much fear that Buhid run indoors and will not venture out again till the next day. The Apnagan elders had brought to our attention that quite a number in the church were unsettled concerning evil spirits. Teaching about the supremacy of Christ over the spiritual world was clearly required to provide assurance that dark forces are powerless against one who exercises trust in Christ.

'How distressing and real!' began Alexandra. After a moment's reflection, she added, 'Do you think your faith is perhaps being tested? Do you believe God is powerful enough to keep you from all harm?'

Inisa was thoughtful for a moment, struggling between a head knowledge of biblical truths and the terror of demons. The reminders of spiritual realities though were appreciated as she nodded her readiness to trust God. Alexandra turned to a favourite text, very appropriate to what Inisa needed to hear at that moment. The Word of God has power to soothe and give peace, providing strength and assurance like no human words ever can.

> … If God is for us, who can be against us? …Who shall separate us from the love of Christ? Shall trouble or

hardship or persecution or famine or nakedness or danger or sword? ... No, in all these things we are more than conquerors through him who loved us. For I am convinced that neither death nor life, neither angels nor demons, neither the present nor the future, nor any powers ... will be able to separate us from the love of God that is in Christ Jesus our Lord. (Rom. 8:31,35,37–39, NIV)

On listening to these verses, Inisa asked where she could reread them at home. After writing down the reference on a scrap of paper, the three of us prayed together, calling upon the strength of the Lord to be with Inisia.

Women on the fringe of the church, as well as those who did not attend, gravitated towards Alexandra, finding they could talk about any manner of thing without being thought unspiritual or lacking maturity. She was very much regarded as one of them, a wife and a mother to whom they could relate, more the friend than the missionary. Alexandra came to deeply appreciate their candour and friendship.

I admired her spontaneity, her ability to rise to any occasion; a quality I often lacked. The two of us made a good team. Through being interdependent, we enjoyed a more far-reaching ministry than either one of us on our own could have had. Alexandra had an eye for the immediate, myself for the mid-term, which although complementary, required respect for the other's outlook. Mutually encouraging of the different gifts developing in one another, eased the pressure of feeling unequal (or unready) to meet a certain need at a given moment.

The hills of Mindoro have no government infrastructure – no roads, electricity, or running water; they are without hospitals or clinics, with no lawyer or police, no professional class. The Buhid have looked to the missionary to provide help in some of these areas. With tribal missionaries being largely people with practical abilities, often marked by an attitude that will give anything a try once, it falls to their lot to be a health worker as well as some of these other professions. The Hanselmans had done a good job, seeing to many of the health needs of the tribe and earned much respect, carried on over to ourselves. Alexandra was prepared to grow into this role and to further develop it, whereas I had the concern that we might perhaps give the wrong medicine and maim or kill someone. I told them that with a laugh on several occasions, but it never prevented them from seeking my medical opinion during the year I was in the hills without Alexandra. Thankfully Alexandra never overdosed anyone or prescribed something very harmful – and we thank God's graciousness in equipping her with an aptitude to acquire a good amount of medical knowledge.

'Kom-kom – I am going to take your blood!' the lowland nurse announced to an elderly tribal man we had brought along to the clinic in Bongabong to be checked over for TB. Kom-kom looked alarmed, already eyeing the exit. It had taken considerable persuasion on his wife's part for Kom-kom to accompany us in the first place.

'Don't be afraid,' interjected Alexandra, 'the nurse is only going to put a cloth band around your arm which will feel a little tight. This will tell the nurse how well your heart is pumping the blood around your body! She won't take any blood from you!'

Getting to the clinic had already been a strange ordeal for Kom-kom as he rode a traysikel for the first time in his life. The poor man never spoke and his eyes flicked around him like an agitated bird.

'How old are you?' the nurse asked Kom-kom.

Kom-kom made no reply.

'The older tribal people don't know their age,' illumined Alexandra.

'Do you remember Japanese soldiers?' I asked him. Kom-kom nodded suspiciously.

'Oh yes I remember the Japanese,' remarked Hagan, another old fellow we had with us. 'I was about this high when we saw them walk along one of our trails!' Hagan held his hand at about waist height and was about to launch off into some lengthy recollection, until I held my hand up slightly. Kom-kom smiled.

'And would you have been about that height?' Alexandra asked Kom-kom.

Without saying anything, Kom-kom held his hand up to his lower chest.

'Let's say that would be about ten years old!' reckoned my wife, who, taxed by anything mathematical, turned to me to work out his probable age.

'Well if he were ten in 1943 for example, that would now make Kom-kom sixty-five!' I calculated at last. The nurse eyed us with bemusement and reluctantly entered sixty-five on the clinic's form. She took his blood pressure and noted the countdown, together with his height and weight, after measuring him on the scales and against a ruler marked on the wall. The same was done for Hagan. We were then told to wait to see the doctor.

The doctor was a kindly faced man, very portly although still in his early thirties. He was very accommodating, allowing the four of us to enter his room for the examination. His manner was not only gracious with us but we were impressed by his extending the same graciousness to our tribal friends, even using the '*Po*', the form of respect when addressing your elders and social superiors, rarely used by lowlanders when relating to tribal folk. He took pains to explain the procedures to our friends and gave them both a small Perspex pot each with a lid for them to collect a sample of sputum first thing in the morning to be tested for TB. The doctor led us back to the receptionist.

'Now you can go for your X-ray,' remarked the nurse, handing a paper to Alexandra. We learned the X-ray machine was not at the clinic, but further down the road.

After a five-minute walk, we came to another public building: a small, private hospital. The receptionist directed us out of the main building, round into the back yard where a number of plywood sheds lined the perimeter. There we found the X-ray department and a young male radiologist.

'Now, the X-ray takes a photograph of what you look like under your skin,' explained Alexandra to our two friends. 'It doesn't hurt,' said my wife, noting Komkom's consternation about the phrase 'under the skin'!

Hagan decided that he would go first, being the slightly more town-wise of the two.

The hut was only large enough to contain the X-ray machine and a table. There was no screen for the radiologist to disappear behind. Instead, he came outside the hut to activate the machine and protect himself from radiation.

'You can come out now!' said the young man to Hagan, poking his head in through the doorway of the hut.

'Is it taken already?' asked Hagan in a most dubious voice. The young man nodded. 'Are you sure?' pursued Hagan.

'Oh yes, the film will be ready in a short while!' said the radiologist now tinkering about with the equipment.

Hagan sidled conspiratorially up to us. 'He seems terribly young!' Hagan said, nodding in the direction of the radiologist. 'Do you think he knows what he is doing?'

'Oh, I should think so,' assured my wife. Hagan still looked unconvinced.

'He looks as though he should still be at school!' continued Hagan, now leaning forward to size the young man up through the doorway. 'Maybe he hasn't been trained yet!'

'What makes you say that?' I asked.

'Well,' Hagan began, sidling back up to us again. In a low voice he explained, 'There was no flash from the photograph equipment and yet he says he took a picture!' We could not help smiling, but saved our laughter until later in the day when we were on our own.

'So where is the other man – what's his name – Kom-kom?' asked the radiologist. We had not noticed Kom-kom was no longer with us as we had tried to allay Hagan's fears. Had the man bolted? Where would he have gone?

It was then that we observed Kom-kom relieving himself against the wall of one of the far huts. My wife engaged the young man with a question or two to try to conceal what Kom-kom was doing on the wall of their new hospital extension. I motioned Kom-kom to return across the yard, thinking that we had perhaps avoided any embarrassment since the radiologist was preoccupied in answering my wife's questions. But the tell-tale mark of a wet patch down the plywood appeared so blatantly obvious.

'Now you need to remove your shirt!' said the radiologist to Kom-kom. The old man quickly obliged.

'Only your shirt is all you need to remove,' added Alexandra, quickly, as Kom-kom was about to remove his loincloth to go completely naked.

The procedure completed, the radiologist passed us two extremely blurred X-rays each of which he carefully placed in a large brown envelope. These had to be taken to a certain doctor's clinic in a different part of town to be interpreted and have a report written up. The report which came back a few days later, recorded 'inconclusive', hardly surprisingly considering the blurred quality of the picture.

We walked back to the town centre and bought our two friends a soft drink apiece and a small bag of assorted breads with sweet coconut fillings. We waited with them until the jeepney was ready to depart. The interior being well filled, the two men agilely clambered up the jeepney's side onto the roof where they sat on the spare wheel. Kom-kom not only lost his worried look, but for the first time that day had a grin from ear to ear! He really must have believed he would not return home; a common assumption made considering so many leave their ailments far too late before hospital treatment in fear of the consequently high mortality rate – or get fatal infections after surgery carried out in less than pristine operating theatres!

Alexandra had wanted to train as a nurse. Cautious at first, she only treated what she was confident with. Armed with the excellent layman's medical manual – *Where there is no Doctor* – specifically dealing with medical matters in the tropics and in a third world environment, Alexandra soon applied herself to treating an increasingly wider range of ailments. She soon handled most primary healthcare matters with a competence that astounded me and with a knowledge of much of the jargon that left me quite speechless and ignorant whenever she got talking medical matters with our mission doctor in Manila.

During our first visit back to Britain after the initial four-year period of being in the Philippines, Alexandra attended a primary healthcare course. Before long into our second term, she was often able to identify and distinguish between the various natures of fever such as, for example, whether someone was suffering from malaria or dengue or typhoid.

The Buhid could only benefit from Alexandra's knowledge when present in their village; this prompted Alexandra to hold interactive health training sessions. Almost always women attended these and judging by the turnout and persistency in attending the meetings, the teaching was much appreciated.

'So what would you say are the more typical illnesses that people suffer from in the village?' Alexandra asked one such group.

'Diarrhoea, that's the most common ailment, especially among our children!' remarked one young mother. She leant forward and let an immense globule of saliva fall to the ground. 'Many of them die from diarrhoea, you know!'

'My husband is always complaining about pains in his stomach a short time after he has eaten!' remarked another woman, who had a child suckling at her breast, its hand tweaking the nipple of the other breast as though it aided the dispensing of the mother's milk. A good number of the other women also said their husbands suffered with ulcers, as did some of the women themselves.

'Do you know why so many of you suffer with ulcers?' asked Alexandra.

'Is it something to do with not eating for a long time and then eating a lot?' replied an older woman. She went on to say that Ligaya had drummed this truth into them; not that it made much difference to the eating habits of the majority. Many went out to their fields in the morning on an empty stomach, maybe ate a pineapple or two as a mid-morning refreshment, or brewed some strong home-grown coffee, and came home ravenous, eating 'a hill of rice', sufficient to feed four or five western adults. The shrunken stomach would suddenly become distended and overburdened.

Having written up a comprehensive list of ailments – from intestinal worms to machete accidents – Alexandra would then ask their opinion as to why they contracted these ailments in the first place (as with the example of the ulcer). This led naturally on to the preventative measures taken to avoid getting sick, which often brought self-realised revelations as they discovered their hunches were often correct. Hunches confirmed made the difference of their being acted upon. Next she quizzed them as to the herbal remedies many of them used, noting that not all the herbal remedies were common knowledge even within a village community and sometimes what was prescribed in one place was not prescribed in another. By collating this information, knowledge was disseminated among the many rather than keeping it confined to just the few. Most of the remedies were sound, God-given medicines.

'What should you do if you have a cut from a *fotol* and the blood is pouring out?' asked one woman.

'You should rub lots of soil into it!' replied her neighbour in a slightly dismissive tone of voice. Frightened by the sight of blood, Buhid panic. Living too far away from the clinic to be stitched up and not even having plasters and bandages to bind such a wound, the idea of rubbing earth into the wound to stem the flow becomes more understandable!

The women were conscientious students, duly noting prescription details down in exercise books balanced on church pews before which they squatted, copying from the chalkboard.

Alexandra sourced a Christian organisation in Manila that retailed medicines at almost ex-factory prices, making many products as much as four to five times cheaper than those purchased in the lowland towns of Mindoro. She bought such quantities that it made me very hot and stressed carrying all the boxes to and from the buses and the boat, jeepneys and traysikels, to bring them to where these were badly needed. Finding a freight company that delivered the medicines within the week from Manila to the door of our landlord's home in Bongabong was a great relief.

Although now affordable to a good many Buhid, these medicine prices were still beyond the means of the poorest families. This prompted Alexandra to properly develop a livelihood project that was already run on an ad hoc basis. Buhid women and many children were very skilled at making woven baskets and pots, containers and purses out of buri, nito, rattan and vine as well as weaving clothes on small looms. Jewellery made out of beads was also in demand by the youth outside of the tribe and beyond the Philippines. Alexandra brought in orders and also bought up extra to sell through the OMF mission homes through which there was a frequent passing of folk from all parts of the world eager to buy souvenirs to take home. A bartering system was enabled, handicrafts for medicines, worked out fairly according to their respective values.

One family sometimes paid us in firewood. Early on with the Buhid, I was surprised by the relatively long distances Buhid carried their firewood when I could find a reasonable supply just beyond the village. One day though when the wind blew the smoke from our cooking fire straight into a couple of neighbouring homes, we heard muttering followed by someone coming out to investigate. Noticing the highly acrid smoke was coming from our fire, the neighbour disappeared and reappeared a short while later with a pile of chopped wood neatly bound up with vine. This wood burnt with smoke that did not smart the eyes so much. We could hear the titters as they related to one another the ignorance of foreigners. Fancy our not knowing that certain wood is not for burning on the cooking fire!

We approved of this sense of pride considering their otherwise low self-esteem. In many things they had an exceedingly superior knowledge; their resourcefulness and ingenuity were truly admirable. A lad of twelve would know how to build his own home, hunt for birds, lay snares, cultivate the land, gather from the rain forest, and generally be able to survive in the jungle with only a *fotol*. Not only biologically able to father a child, he was already practically prepared having to bring up younger siblings whilst parents were tending their fields. An outsider would not last a week in the jungle for all his academic learning!

One afternoon when Alexandra was having a chat with a number of women on the balcony of our Batangan home, an elderly lady came to the foot of the steps leading up to where the others were seated. She hesitated, possibly due to her great age and arthritis.

'It's still wide up here!' said my wife, a Buhid greeting of welcome, indicating there was still plenty of space to seat the newcomer.

The old lady slowly came up the five steps and joined the others. Her name was Gino'o, one of the first believers in this village who had outlived her husband, contrary to the norm since women, having so many children, were unlikely to outlive their husbands. Gino'o now lived with her son-in-law, too old to ever venture far from home these days.

Gino'o surreptitiously carried with her an old plastic bag containing a few home-made baskets. After a good ten minutes during which she did not participate at all in the conversation, she nudged Mina, a thirty-something mum sitting beside her, too embarrassed to negotiate her business herself. Mina came over to sit beside my wife, removed four rattan containers and placing these down on the space on the bench between them. They were the wonkiest woven goods we ever saw.

Some of the women on the balcony chuckled, not unkindly, upon seeing Gino'o's efforts, nudging others who were not yet aware of what was then taking place. They knew Alexandra had a strict code of practice, accepting only a high standard of work to ensure quality control of handicrafts that had to be saleable in Manila and to foreign buyers. Several of these women had had their own work, considerably superior to that of Gino'o's, rejected. The question on all of their minds was obviously: What was she going to say to Gino'o?

'Were you not wearing your glasses when you made these?' Mina asked the old woman. The black nito strands used in forming a design upon the straw-coloured rattan was all askew, highlighting the unintentionally crooked shape of each of the containers.

Gino'o's laugh trailed off into a series of guttural chuckles. Her face puckered up, and crazed into 100 lines of humour. Her skin resembled an ancient porcelain vase criss-crossed with a filigree of cracks.

'Maybe you need another pair of spectacles,' suggested another woman in a good-hearted tease.

The pregnant pause created a sense of mounting anticipation. Onak and her friend already having a fit of suppressed giggles, were unable to contain themselves longer and openly laughed, making others follow suit. Gino'o sat there amongst all these younger women, her bright orange bead hairband showing vividly against the grey-white of her hair. Something almost regal was in her mien; unabashed to be wearing the blue tribal blouse in spite of it being in great need of a launder and a fair number of stitches, Gino'o sat there stoically indifferent to the teases of her juniors.

'I will give you 15 pisos for each one,' announced Alexandra who never had the heart to turn down anything that Gino'o made. We knew she was destitute and could use the money to buy herself some food treats from the eateries on the main street. This way Gino'o had the dignity of seemingly earning the money without it striking her as being charity, a point conveyed to the other women once Gino'o had disappeared.

Alexandra gathered up the wonky wonders in her hands without bothering with the greasy polythene they had come in and placed these inside on top of a cabinet where more of Gino'o's unsaleable work was positioned. They were always useful for keeping clothes pegs and coins and strips of tablets and the like in. We had more of these lopsided containers in our Bongabong base house, still useful although of little aesthetic value. What they lacked in finesse they made up for in character and these baskets were daily reminders of this elderly soul of whom we were very fond.

Alexandra would often visit Gino'o in her home. A corner of her son-in-law's house seemed to be hers. She was almost always ensconced there, leaning against the wall in the gloom, looking wistfully out of the far window. She had a pet crow, as bedraggled-looking as herself, reared from a chick. Some of the tribal lads had brought this chick from one of their hunting expeditions. After a lengthy debate as to who would best care for this orphan bird, they had brought it to Gino'o, reasoning that since she was always at home and had nothing better to do, she was the obvious choice.

The crow had an exceptionally sullen disposition towards all except its mistress. It had its place in the home on the end of a bamboo bed, pecking at anyone who came within striking distance of its perch, or so much as dared to sit on any part of the bed. Even before you came near, the bird warned you of its presence with a raucous croak and continued to complain about your intrusion into the tranquillity of their home until Gino'o reprimanded it. Gino'o was the only person it respected and obeyed, for anyone else in that household who tried to discipline the crow would be given an earful until they desisted. Iain, who has a passion for birds, always enjoyed visiting Gino'o. He and his sister would jokingly remark, 'Are we going to see the old crow?' in a delightful ambiguity. Like everyone else, Iain kept a respectful distance from the crow, yet could never take his admiring eyes off it, for scruffy though it may have been, it certainly had character.

In enabling the health project to finally get underway, the Buhid were to elect a healthcarer from among them, one in each village; one who was not a recent convert, who showed a mature prayer life as well as having an aptitude for diagnosing the illness and prescribing the appropriate medicine. All too aware that the bringing in of these medicines might throw out the ways of faith, we did not wish them to dispense with their natural recourse to pray for healing.

'Tell me about all the children you have given birth to,' Alexandra asked of a typical forty-year-old Buhid mother.

'My first child was a boy. We named him Abraham, but he did not live long for he suffered badly from asthma and died during an attack. Next was a girl – Yomai. She is married and lives on the other side of Batangan with three children of her own. The third child was a premature birth at eight months. I had tripped on a langka tree root and lost my balance in the mud. The baby did not live beyond a couple of days. My fourth child is Maling who plays guitar in the church. I reckon he is twenty-two years old and of course isn't married yet.' The mother broke off with a laugh which she concealed behind her hand, indicating she thought it time he took a wife.

'The fifth one is another girl, Yomie, who is a househelp to a Luktanon family in Manila. We haven't had news of her for nearly a year now and I worry about her as there are many bad things that go on in that city. Then there is Nehemias, the boy who is always off trapping songbirds. He doesn't talk a great deal, except to his birds. He is about sixteen and is being noticed now by the girls.' Again the mother broke off with a sense of shyness at revealing these personal details. Soon she continued again, glad to relate to someone who was showing an interest in her family.

'My seventh child we called "Baby". When pregnant with her, I had a bad bout of malaria and was given strong medicines for this at the clinic near Roxas. That was a difficult time in the midst of a famine and we were often very short of food. We had to work hard and walk far to find enough to eat. Baby was born with a deformed head probably due to the malaria medicines. I had little breast milk at times and Baby's hunger often was not satisfied. She died during mango season. She had only been born when we were preparing our land.'

'You prepare your land around about February, don't you, and mango season isn't until about October, is it?' remarked Alexandra. 'So that made Baby only eight months old when she died.'

'Yes, that would be about right. My next child was very different. He was big, a really healthy-looking one that you thought would survive anything. He died after only one week. Maybe he had a heart problem? Or maybe he got trodden on by my other children in the house as they would often play inside the house during the rainy season!

'The next one is a girl, who is now about nine years old. We called her Sindy, named after the newsreader on the Christian radio station. How many is that now?'

'Sindy would be your ninth child,' remarked Alexandra as she noted all these details down in a notebook, something we both did to try to learn some of the names of the children now teeming in the Christian villages where infanticide was no longer practised.

'Well that brings me to Malakias – he is about eight and healthy. Then next is Zefanias, another healthy boy, about six years old. And last of all is this one here,' she dangled a three-month-old boy on her lap, naked except for a grubby vest much soiled by a running nose. 'So is that 12 children you have written down?' asked the mother, leaning over the notebook.

'Yes, 12. Four of them have died and eight are still living!'

This was an average ratio; one out of every three children were likely never to reach adulthood, the majority of them dying in their formative months, often from dehydration resulting from diarrhoea and vomiting, others being taken away by measles.

Chapter Nine:

At Sea with Moses

'What is Monay bringing?' Alexandra asked Talad, Monay's wife; this couple were very effectively leading the Batangan church.

Seated on the floor of her home, Talad agilely turned her body round and lent against the doorpost to see what Monay had brought. Arriving all sweaty and very grubby from the hills, Monay carefully put down an eight-foot section of a broad tree trunk. The trunk was obviously not intended for firewood, as he had lowered it to the ground carefully. Even from the twenty or so feet distance between Monay and ourselves, the trunk was evidently very rotten.

Talad laughed generously and with warmth, latterly covering her mouth with her hand as was considered polite among the Luktanon. Monay and Talad spoke very good Tagalog having both graduated from the Bible school up north. Amongst the Buhid, this couple were positively cosmopolitan, yet retaining their tribal identity as we were about to see.

'Are there many?' Talad asked her husband, not deliberately ignoring Alexandra's question but rather ascertaining the facts before elucidating. Monay replied monosyllabically as one still used to spending the best part of the day on his own in the hills. Having fetched a wok from the kitchen, Monay was stripping away the easily removable bark from the rotten log and was picking out white globules as large as the end joint of one's thumb.

Knowing the ways of outsiders – Luktanon and foreigner alike – Talad became embarrassed and laughed. Scratching her head roughly and with her customary broad grin showing many missing teeth, Talad replied to my wife's question, 'These are the maggots of a large beetle!'

With that bit of information and reading the unease that Talad's body language conveyed, I realised they planned to eat these maggots. Talad evidently thought it unsophisticated to eat such things. My wife, either slow at realising what they were about, or perhaps more out of a sense of wanting to put Talad at ease, expressed interest, continuing with her questioning.

'What are you going to do with the grubs?' she asked with warm enthusiasm.

Talad laughed again, louder this time, causing her to throw back her head. She confirmed my thoughts.

'And do you eat them raw or cook them first?' continued my wife. The increased interest did make Talad feel more at ease, since we had not just reacted with disgust; however, I felt more unsettled as the explanations unfolded.

'We like to cook them first, but you can eat them raw.'

Alexandra and I had already been with Talad for over half an hour and I was eager to speak with Monay about his forthcoming trip across the island to the village where he and Talad had served as missionaries.

'And how do you cook the maggots?' I groaned inwardly at where all this expressed interest was going to lead, amazed by my wife's insistence not to drop the subject. Surely she was aware that such interest was bound to lead to our being invited to partake of this tribal delicacy? Enthused by Alexandra's interest, Talad rose to her feet.

'Come on, and I'll show you,' Talad invited my wife over to the kitchen lean-to section of their hut. Crouching down on her haunches, Talad scraped away a pile of ash between the tripod of stones upon which pans were balanced to cook, and blew upon the charred remains of the lunchtime fire. A slight glow lit the gloom of the hut as she gathered the remnants into a small pile, adding a few thin wood shavings. Once these ignited she placed kindling sticks on the fire and later, more substantially sized wood.

I joined Monay outside as he stripped away all the remaining bark from the tree, totally depopulating the log of its healthy, fat inhabitants.

'Have you planted your maize yet?' I asked.

'I've made a start. A few more days now and it will be finished.' Monay looked up whilst answering me.

'That's good. Quite a few are still preparing their land. I saw three or four fires smoking away earlier over the Matanos River way.'

'That will probably be Habid. He told me after this morning's prayer meeting that he was going there to slash and burn.' Monay grinned, picked out another three maggots before adding, 'And Antak too. I met him going with his son across the Matanos earlier.'

'When are you planning to go to Datag Bonglay?' I ventured after further small talk, coming to the subject I had been waiting to talk about.

'Soon,' he replied, not so much elusively but rather in the manner of one reckoning to himself when such a trip across the island to his former mission ground would be made. 'Maybe before the coming weekend.'

By now Monay had stripped the rotten log clean of bark and not a maggot remained. He brought these through to the kitchen in a very old, rusty wok. Talad already had another wok on the fire, a newer one thoroughly blackened by the cooking fires on the outside but scoured clean to the metal on the inside with shingle from the stream. Into this she poured a little oil from an old soya sauce bottle, waiting a little while for it to come up to heat before grabbing a handful of maggots which she tossed into the pan. The fat creatures writhed and squirmed briefly before becoming motionless, entwined in a golden shroud as the oil fried them crisp.

Whilst this cooking preparation was underway, Monay beckoned me to come back in to the main part of the house, up on the raised, split bamboo floor. Alexandra popped her head around the entrance to announce she was off, with a smile that I alone knew expressed a certain pleasure at landing me in it.

'Stay and have some grubs,' Talad tried to entice my wife.

'No, I really must be on my way. Dahlia will be searching for me to have her leg wound dressed. She failed to come yesterday and her mother said she would send her over to our house this afternoon. I should have gone sooner!'

Too right, I thought to myself, she should have left before all the expressed interest in the maggots. My hosts were leading up to the inevitable invitation to partake of this fatty feast. My wife swanned blissfully away.

'Are you interested in joining me?' Monay asked. I shivered within, thinking he was referring to this snack. With there being no plate of maggots before us, I looked him quizzically in the face.

'We could walk across the island this Friday and spend the weekend in Datag Bonglay and remain there halfway into next week.'

I was hesitant, prompting Monay to explain further.

'Sometime on Thursday afternoon – that is tomorrow – we could leave for Siyangi and spend the night there and make an early start for Occidental on the Friday.' He enthused the more as he planned this visit.

Datag Bonglay is an epic walk from Siyangi, the nearest church in the east – a distance of some 40 miles through very mountainous terrain. This Mindoro trans-island trail, one of several, goes up a long valley with a river difficult to cross when in spate between June to December, before ascending the central dividing mountain chain in the region of 5,000 feet.

'There are boulders strewn across the several mountain ridges so immense they require you to leap from one to the next!' Monay warmed to the adventure.

'How long does the walk take?' I asked.

'If you walk from Siyangi the length of time it takes for a pot of rice to be cooked, the first light of dawn will then appear in the eastern sky!' Monay's father spoke. He had come back from his land a short while before, and was lying out flat. Although into his early sixties, his muscular body glistening with sweat, had not an ounce of flab.

'If you keep on walking,' the father proceeded, now propping himself up on an elbow, 'and are not lazy to have rests, you will just manage to reach Datag Bonglay as the sun is setting ahead of you.'

In our terms this approximated to a 12-hour walk. I have experienced such a pace as he referred to. Uphill, whatever the gradient, is a determined stride, and downhill, a mad, mad chase sometimes using a staff as a third leg to enable gigantic leaps. They urge and spur one another on with lively banter at times and with whoops of delight as they career down the mountainsides, anxious to keep up with the fastest.

Suffering from heat exhaustion in more than 90 degrees Fahrenheit, combined with the high humidity, we had never been fit enough to consider this walk, especially after I had contracted TB (which, although I was cured of, had left me weakened).

'We could camp the night in the mountains to break the distance down into a two-day walk,' Monay thoughtfully suggested, responding to my spoken misgivings. Even half the distance was still far longer than we had ever walked in the tropics. Derek – a very fit colleague of ours – took three days to do a very similar journey over this same trans-island pass. Not anticipating being on the trail for a third day, his tribal party had run out of food on the second day. Derek had struggled to make it through, very much the worse for wear with leech bites turning into tropical ulcers. The NPA further complicated the great traverse, especially with a foreigner in tow. This was their territory and a substantial detour would have to be made if we learned of one of their camps en route.

'Help yourself!' said Talad. For a short while I had quite forgotten the fairly imminent invitation to try a fried maggot. Now a plate was set before us. I could have declined but that would have set me apart even more as not only the foreigner unable to endure the tropical heat of a long, long walk, but as the outsider who wouldn't even try their food – especially something they considered a delicacy.

I really ought to try one, I persuaded myself. Just because I was not brought up on this diet didn't mean it wouldn't be palatable, I continued to reason internally. After all, I just might be discovering some new culinary delight.

I could not refuse to take the largest and juiciest-looking specimen from Monay's hand. Gamely I took hold of it, remembering the joke of a missionary's prayer: 'Lord, I will get it down if you keep it down.' Not daring to take it whole, I bit into the body that had surprising resistance, its wrinkled skin having been made crisp in the wok. Suddenly my teeth broke through the outer layer and the fatty mass of maggot slowly oozed with toothpaste-like consistency onto my tongue. This was not something to be savoured but to be swallowed promptly and with that in mind, I popped the other half of the maggot into my mouth. I should have just swallowed it whole for as it lay upon my tongue it seemed to have doubled in volume. I thought I might possibly choke. I chewed upon the half-formed platelets making up its beetle-forming body, concluding these were as unchewable as thin strips of plastic. The fatty flesh tasted reminiscent of paraffin! I don't know if it was supposed to taste like that or whether the maggot had been contaminated with a smear of the fuel from either the plate or Monay's hand, but I didn't pick out a second one to determine if this was just a freak. Worst of all was a leg, yes a leg, that I dislodged from between my teeth! This creature was obviously well evolved, the pick of the choice as far as Monay was concerned. I swallowed with difficulty, my throat protesting to the texture although this natural aversion was probably more a protest of the mind rather than throat. The brain however continued to suggest rejection to all other fellow parts of my digestive anatomy.

At that moment I did not think well of my wife, and come to that, I certainly did not feel that well in myself either. I politely declined the second maggot swiftly offered me on noticing how quickly I had eaten the first, and having the urge to retch, I quickly wound up our conversation as naturally as I could.

'Yes, Friday would be possible for me to come to Datag Bonglay. However, I won't join you on the walk over as I would hold you up too much but I will ask Moses if he would like to come with me in an outrigger canoe around the coast and we can meet up on the other side of the island. I tell you what, I will go and ask him now before he fixes anything else up for this weekend.'

With that I was up on my feet to the surprise of my hosts who unsuccessfully tried to detain me further with the offer of another maggot or two. They agreeably concluded that it was well I should approach Moses now rather than later.

My stomach heaved as I briskly walked away. I managed to contain the contents in my mouth until I was a respectable distance from the house. Back at our hut, before proceeding to Moses' place, I brushed my teeth more than once to get rid of all taste of the fatty substance with the trace of paraffin flavour. My wife looked on with a mixture of giggles and concern.

That Friday, Moses and I boarded the early morning jeepney leaving Batangan at seven. The jeepney was crowded as usual with school children all dressed in white shirts, the girls wearing hand-me-down maroon skirts, faded and often-repaired, and the lads with long black trousers. The slim girls, some with their long dark hair still wet from an early morning bathe, rode inside with the overweight Luktanon women with their short-cropped hair. These latter were the owners of corner stores and eating houses, off to Roxas for fresh provisions. School lads, larking about, full of jokes and wisecracks, rode precariously on the roof with men equipped with *fotols* off to hire themselves out as labourers to Luktanon farmers, sitting on top of the bamboo poles, sacks of copra and charcoal. The roof creaked under all the weight. With Filipino-made vehicles being unequipped with handbrakes – such equipment is considered a non-essential accessory – the boulders that had been placed under the wheels to prevent the jeepney from rolling away were removed. Another eighteen or twenty men mounted the narrow ledge running along the chassis base on either side, giving the jeepney a porcupine appearance, bristling with men leaning out from the sides.

This first trip of the day almost always left punctually, ensuring the students would arrive at Morente in time for their classes. Beyond Morente, spare seats were to be had in the jeepney and more room too for those still clinging to the sides to gain a more comfortable perch for hands and feet. Leaving the jeepney at the junction of the southbound highway, Moses and I boarded another vehicle, a hybrid version between a jeepney and a bus, and paid fares to take us all the way to journey's end at Bulalacao. I had only travelled part of this route twice before, so much of the scenery was new. Travelling unknown ways was an enjoyment which Moses likewise shared.

The tribal lands of the Hanunoo Mangyan did not look as appealing as the territory the Buhid enjoyed to the north. The hills were lower and brown as we were well into dry season, their slopes largely denuded of forest. The region was dusty and often looked barren, the more so the further south we travelled, with empty makeshift market stalls along the wayside adding to the air of abandonment. I appreciated why Hanunoo marrying Buhid usually settled in the more fertile and forested lands of the Buhid.

Bulalacao was reached towards late morning, the only sizeable town encountered for miles around. The small port lent a mercantile feel to the town's cluster of eateries and brightly-painted concrete stores, selling electrical goods. Its prosperous air contrasted with the bamboo and coco lumber of many of the villages passed through en route. Bulalacao links Oriental and Occidental Mindoro provinces by a passenger *bangka* connection as well as a rough track that in recent times had been driveable right through to San Jose over in the west.

However, the road was closed due to landslides caused by the heavy seasonal rains.

Having bought tickets for the 1.30 passenger *bangka* bound for San Jose, Moses and I went in search of an eatery. *Bangkas* are outrigger canoes, which these days are largely equipped with outboard motors. They range considerably in size from the precarious one-man version to a sturdy vessel carrying forty or so passengers. We finally settled for the eatery beside the pier from where we could see our *bangka* come in and be ready in case it decided to leave sooner than anticipated. The *karinderia*, as such eateries are known in the Philippines, displayed many large aluminium pots along the front of the counter containing the *ulam* – the accompaniment eaten with a plate of rice. Most of these were fish stews, plainly boiled. Fish fried a long time ago had a vulcanised appearance, some smothered in a sweet and sour sauce. For the non-fish lover like myself, tired of the fish-head stews of the Mangyan, there were the pork dishes – *adobo* stewed in vinegar and soya sauce; *afritada* prepared in a sweet and thick tomato ketchup-type sauce. All these accompaniments were served cold or at best, lukewarm and washed down with an ice-cold soft drink.

Many passengers for the 1.30 trip to San Jose had the same idea as ourselves, and ate in the pier *karinderia* wanting to be on hand for the arrival of the *bangka*. We were glad to be close by, for everyone in the *karinderia* was waiting for the same *bangka*, and from experience, possessing a ticket did not necessarily guarantee a place on the trip. If the *bangka* could fill up beforehand, it could leave without waiting for the departure time, especially should the weather favour an earlier start. Quite a wind was blowing and whilst the water looked choppy about the wharf, it certainly did not yet give one second thoughts. Way out to sea though, beyond the lea of the long peninsula stretching out a mile or two due south, the sea's surface looked troubled, crested with white horses.

Moses looked a little anxious.

'I can't swim!' he confessed, something not at all unusual among Filipinos – although somewhat surprising considering they never live that far from the sea on any one of their 7,000 islands.

'But didn't I see you swimming in the Siyangi River last year?'

'Oh yes, I can swim about in a river as you are rarely out of your depth nor ever far from the bank – but the sea...' I patted him on the back saying he would be fine. If he were to fall overboard for example at least he could tread water till the *bangka* circled back to him, or he could swim the few strokes to latch on to an outrigger arm.

The *bangka* came in, larger than any *bangka* I had ever seen, complete with an enclosed cabin in the centre where passengers could sit out of the weather on a slatted bamboo floor. The boat even had a toilet, a half barrel cubicle suspended over the side of the stern providing privacy only when squatting low; a privacy dependent too upon your fellow passengers keeping a discreet distance, for those using it had their head and shoulders in view. I thought how embarrassing it would be should you suffer from constipation. At least it didn't stink for without drain or toilet bowl, the toilet was constructed to the simplest design conceivable – a hole in the floor looking straight into the sea.

Over thirty people rose from their tables in the *karinderia* and made for the jetty where still more gathered for the *bangka*. We joined the uneasy crowd, wondering whether there would be room for us all on board. No one talked or so much looked at their neighbour. That way it felt less awkward stopping another from stepping on board in front of you. We need not have worried for there was room for all seated Filipino style, cheek by jowl on the cabin floor or shoulder to shoulder leaning over the gunwale.

True to our earlier suspicions, the *bangka* did leave before time for quite a wind was blowing up. On the leeward side of the barren southern peninsula, the sea was unsettled but as we put more distance between ourselves and that hilly spit of land, the swell grew and tossed the *bangka* like a cork. The stern was lifted clear out of the sea making the engine pitch rise dramatically. The giant bamboo making up the outrigger arms groaned under the strain as the boat tried to pitch from side to side. The outrigger was indeed sturdy, made of several bamboo bound together with thick nylon cord with the added reinforcement of thick sawn planks placed across the central section with the bamboo.

While reaching for a piece of rigging blowing free in the wind, a deckhand overreached himself and, passing the point of no return, toppled head-first into the sea. The deckhand was a long way behind us in no time at all, a small head in a large swell, alarmingly disappearing from view by the time word was passed to the captain. It seemed to take an age to turn the *bangka* about, struggling as it moved broadside to the waves before we were on a rescue course. Passengers craned their necks and shielded their eyes from the sun, intently trying to locate the missing person. Many of us feared the worse. It was quite likely that the man overboard was unable to swim.

Thankfully the man came into view, treading water, extreme relief written on his face as he took hold of the outrigger and dragged himself along the thick bamboo arm to reach the body of the *bangka*. The tense episode that had seemed an age for us who were safe on board, made me wonder how long those few minutes had seemed to the deckhand.

I reflected upon what I consider divine protection through all sorts of situations. Once Alexandra had cause to be thankful for being bitten by fiery red ants when sitting on the toilet seat at our Batangan home! The ants had warned her of the need for caution and on a subsequent night, there on the toilet seat, illuminated in the torch light, was a scorpion!

We had also been delivered from harm when we were caught in the midst of a riot at Batangas port. The crowd had been incensed by a multinational consortium's plans to expand considerably into the surrounding squatter communities. This entailed the demolition of a shanty town and the relocation of the poor a good way inland, a solution passionately opposed by a community dependent upon a fishing livelihood. We had just disembarked from the Mindoro ferry and were approaching the port exit to find the gates closed. The police stood back in a line with guns at the ready, nervously watching the swelling crowd shout their protests and occasionally hurl rocks and bottles towards them.

We prayed, cautiously, looking over to the gate. Two Filipino civilians from the port side went up to the exit and passed through. I responded to an inner urge that we too should go up to the gate, not pausing to consider how wise it would be for *Amerikanos* to approach a mob outraged at being ousted by foreign developers. Although the crowd's mood had in no way abated, the missiles had for the moment, and we reached the gates unscathed. The gates just opened before us and the mob on the other side parted enough to allow us through. No one noticed us; a quite extraordinary thing in the Philippines where a foreigner's passing is always greeted with the customary 'Hey Joe!' or by someone shouting out *'Amerikano'* or *'Kano'* for short. Midway through the crowd, Hannah piped up, 'My shoelace has come undone!'

'Just keep on walking, Hannah!' Alexandra said, assertively. We emerged on the far side of the crowd, not only unscathed, but unnoticed. Had God made those Filipinos blind to our identity as he had done to the Arameans when they came to arrest Elisha?

And now, here I was in a precarious vessel, probably overloaded, inadequate for the stormy conditions, rolling and pitching on a swell that soaked anyone not under the cover of the cramped cabin. Many, like Moses, were nervous and others vomited. I reminded myself of the one who had called me and is in control. I felt consoled that I wasn't going to be lost at sea because God's attention was elsewhere, yet I accepted that should disaster befall us, it would be no accident of misfortune.

Reassuringly the *bangka* stayed reasonably close to shore all trip, close enough at least to make out a mountainous coastline studded with deserted coves and many small islands swaying with coconut palms. The fine sandy bays invited me to return some other day when a weekend was free, an opportunity regrettably never taken.

San Jose is a considerable port for the size of the place, having commerce with Palawan and other islands of the western Visayan island group. We all filled a jeepney stationed close to the pier which took us to the town's market and jeepney terminus for the final leg of our journey.

'The last trip left half an hour ago!' a swarthy man informed us with a couldn't-care-less indifference. He seemed to be the 'station-master' but the official designation was not obvious, dressed as he was in a very loose-fitting red vest and shorts, smoking a cigarette which he never removed from his mouth.

'And what about a tricycle – are there any other passengers that would want to share a ride?' asked Moses.

'It would cost you!' the red-vested man ominously replied. 'You wouldn't reach the road end until sunset and with no passengers for the return trip and travelling on the roads being dangerous after dark, it would cost upward of 1,000 pisos!'

That was a week's earnings for the average lowlander out in the provinces so we did not linger to negotiate, particularly since no tricycle driver was about at that moment. Probably my presence inflated the price. We had no further joy in asking some tricycle drivers down the road and resigned ourselves to staying the night in the largest town on all Mindoro, though it did not have the status of even being a provincial capital.

Some streets later, as we moved out of the town centre into the suburbs, we took a twin-bedded room in a place that had the appearance of a student boarding house. Cheap, with no frills whatsoever, laundered jeans and T-shirts hung from packaging string which festooned the corridors. Moses had a big grin as he stood by our room door. Spotting the light switch, he flicked it on. The bare ceiling light bulb shone dimly. Moses switched it off again. Still afternoon, the light was not needed, so I was surprised when Moses switched it back on, then off again. I looked at him quizzically. He was grinning all the more now, still with his hand on the switch as he flicked it up and down another couple of times.

Electricity was something we did not have in Batangan at that time and so the light was an exciting novelty, one that Moses was now in control of. More novelties were in store. Five minutes later, Moses returned from the bathroom with what had become a perpetual grin from ear to ear.

'There are taps!' he said with the delight of one new to a first-class hotel, who might announce there to be a swimming pool, gym or sauna. My disappointment at having missed the last trip was now tempered by my companion's thrill at sampling the high life of San Jose. 'The taps work too. Just screw the handle round and a good flow of clean water comes gushing out – do you not want to come and have a look?'

I did not have the heart to tell him that we had taps in our base house in Bongabong and had grown up with these modern conveniences. Nevertheless I followed Moses down the labyrinth of gloomy corridors that had not seen a lick of paint from the time the hotel had been built twenty or so years ago. Because he lacked any other impressionable companion, I did my best to share Moses' delight with all the taps and lights.

That evening I decided to treat my very amiable friend to the best food the town could offer and ordered a miniature banquet of several dishes to go with our rice. The Mangyan eat a colossal quantity of rice and when the waitress brought us a small mound each, the out-turned contents of a cup, I ordered a further four cupfuls. Moses was satisfied beyond words as he sampled all the different tastes, eating such huge quantities of rice that more had to be ordered.

Early the next day we made it to Datag Bonglay on the first jeepney and met up with our Batangan companions who had walked the gruelling 12-hour trans-island trail. Never having met any of the Buhid in Datag Bonglay before, I was introduced by Monay as, 'Martin is one of us – he eats what we eat!' That was the first time I was glad I had eaten that maggot. Thankfully maggots were never on the menu that week but precious little else was available during dry season in Occidental when near-famine conditions existed for a few weeks. Fewer meals were eaten than usual and a dry starchy yam was our sole diet. I felt guilty eating, being so much better nourished than any of our hosts, particularly the main elder of the community in whose house we were accommodated. He had a pitiful skin condition, so itchy that the skin was peeling away from almost his entire body; and in places was growing a new, very pink layer in stark contrast to his tanned limbs.

During the few days spent there, the small community stopped working and gave themselves to the four daily worship meetings held in their short shed of a church. They were encouraged to be joined by about twenty other Buhid who had hiked the long way over from Siyangi. The singing was spirited and their attention to the teaching was marked by a people hungry for a feast after months living on a subsistence diet.

The novelty of that time over in the west remained forever with Moses, his enjoyment greatly adding to my own. Four years later, I visited Moses when he was suffering from Hepatitis B; then, he was distant with me, embarrassed by my coming to his home. Circumstances had so changed in this young man's life. He had fallen foul of many of his former friends and family. This was the second time he had suffered from Hepatitis, an illness that was making him weaker by the day. Unable to have enough strength to work his land, Moses had turned to stealing, a vice seriously frowned upon in an otherwise very morally tolerant tribal culture. He denied what many confirmed he did. Having turned his back on the church, he was not thrilled by the missionary visiting him.

Only when I came to reminisce about our night in San Jose, did I see a light in his eye. As I reminisced, appealing to him not to forsake all he formerly held dear, including the Lord, he suddenly pressed his forehead onto my shoulder and wept bitterly with convulsions. I have never seen a grown man weep like this. He owned up to all he was accused of and, praying earnestly, asked the Lord's forgiveness. The mention of that night in San Jose had crushed his stony resolve, bringing to mind, too, days when he liked to read God's Word and go to conferences. In spite of getting him to Calapan a couple of days later for diagnostic tests and medicine, Moses was dead within the week of my calling upon him.

Chapter Ten:

At Home in Manihala

'We don't have the money to buy these things,' protested Deborah.

'They're a gift from our church back in Scotland, along with the guitar we brought! If you can arrange for some of the others to come along to the church this afternoon, I will show you various ways of keeping the children's attention.'

My wife spoke with a certain confidence because this package had already been a great success with other churches; not only with the children, but with adults too, who had never had coloured pencils and felts before. The gift of £100 had bought four guitars and four packs of teaching materials and accessories, providing a year's worth of lessons. It formed a tangible link between these churches of the 'highlanders' of Mindoro (the meaning of the word 'Buhid'), with our church in the Scottish Highlands. The teaching package also contained stories and songs, dramas and games, all linked in with the theme of the main point being conveyed. It required much involvement as well as imagination.

In the Batangan Church I had been coerced into helping out with one of these training sessions. I was to lead a team of children around the church, all pretending to be the Good Shepherd looking for the 100th sheep that had gone missing. Some of the older children thought it a silly lark, pretending to find a sheep that was not even real, and therefore could not be found. On the verge of their giving up, I came across a piglet snouting in the dust under one of the church pews. Quickly I grabbed the squealing, writhing animal with one dextrous move that I was proud of, never having handled a piglet before.

The children were delighted. Something that had just been a timely coincidence, perhaps made them wonder whether the piglet had appeared as part of a well-planned programme. The children gleefully anticipated this new teaching approach, replacing tedious sessions run under threat of disciplinary action. They squirmed to reflect on the interminable verse by verse expositions that they had to sit through, taught by those struggling to understand the complex theology of Romans for themselves.

For a few seconds I was surrounded by delighted children all putting a hand on the errant piglet, children who otherwise never took any notice of such a common sight, even in church. They jostled to be by my side until it dawned on them that this was just a drama to illustrate a point. Over the following days whenever I went round visiting folk, I enjoyed an almost celebrity status as children pointed me out to their friends and in whispers named me as the one who had caught the piglet! I never succeeded though in repeating the climax to that particular drama in all the other churches where it was re-enacted.

Sunday schools were transformed through having this structured package. They suddenly became hugely popular. It still beats me how those previous, unstructured sessions had ever succeeded in drawing the children in the first place. I suspect the saving grace had been the children's love of singing. They gave themselves with great gusto to loud and joyful singing and to memorising Bible verses, which they took a great pride in repeating. Greater variety of games, drama and drawings was bound to be a success.

Perched on the side of a hill ridge, a few hundred feet up, looking out to sea, Manihala was a village of about twenty houses. Some houses were scattered, lost from view in banana groves or over the rise. It was a notorious place for mosquitoes at night.

'They can drain a man dry in a night!' exclaimed Kawkaw's father on a visit from his village high up in the hills where mosquitoes were not a problem. The banana groves were breeding grounds for the larvae, where pools of water could gather in between leaf and trunk or on the shady ground beneath, not scorched by the sun. The groves also provided shade during the day for the mosquitoes to escape the glare of the sun they so dislike, by lying low in the dead fronds hanging dry and limp against the trunk of the plant.

Water was sufficient for mosquitoes to breed, but certainly there was a shortage for people. In rainy season, a muddy pool had been scooped out in a storm channel, adequate for foot washing and if desperate, for bathing the body too. But to get a proper wash involved half an hour's hot walking along an undulating hill ridge to a hose pipe! This local initiative in conjunction with the Luktanon hill farmers, provided portable water to an extensive community scattered on either side of the lengthy hill ridge. The hose was run from a clear spring some distance away. Sometimes a queue formed whilst one filled large five-gallon plastic containers and another, having a strip wash, stood all lathered up on a sawn plank, momentarily clean until having to step off the mudless platform into the quagmire beyond – all caused by having a hose running continually. Sometimes in rainy season, when these hills were a great mud bath, we returned home from our bathe at the hose in a worse state than when we had set out!

Literacy classes were run for a good number in the church building twice daily, giving the gratification that by the end of the week many had really been encouraged by their unexpected progress and determined to persevere after we left the village. Some attending were already quite proficient but enjoyed coming together to improve on these skills. We pitched the teaching at those who most needed help; this did not seem to dampen the ardour of those who were already fairly literate. When I came round to check the copying of the Bible verses from the blackboard, the women giggled, covering up their efforts momentarily out of shyness before permitting me to look at their work. They warmed to encouragement, something they had not encountered in these learning situations before. Awang, one of the really literate men who just enjoyed sitting in to observe my teaching approach, could not contain himself any longer: 'You know, you are so very different from the teachers in the school. You are so kind and explain ways of identifying what the letters are. I never had a teacher like that at school!'

This comment opened my eyes to how children could be written off as being slow and stupid, to the extent that they believed themselves incapable of learning to read and write and gave up, like so many of them seemed to have done. Fatalistically accepting they were born plain stupid, they did not entertain any further aspirations about any possible intellectual potential. This in part explained why the likes of Gano were labelled as illiterate and no one bothered to try and teach them again.

Gano acted as our host whenever we came to Manihala. I knew Gano's brothers who lived in Siyangi and, knowing them to be literate, endowed with sharp minds, I asked Gano why he had never learned to read and write.

'I went to school for two years!' he replied, fondly recalling the experience. I pursued the matter as to why he had not learned to read.

'Well, there always seemed more interesting things happening about me. An aeroplane would fly past and I would be over at the window watching it fly from one end of the sky to the other. Usually something was happening out of the window, a dog wandering about, a bird perching upon a branch or other children at play... you know the kind of thing – I was easily distracted!'

'Did your teacher never get annoyed with you for not paying attention?' I ventured.

'No,' he smiled, wistfully, 'I was the teacher's pet. If anything needed fetching from another classroom, or a note had to be taken to the head teacher, or if my teacher wanted a rice cake from the street vendor, I was the one sent. No, my teacher was very pleased with me!'

Looking at his kind, good-mannered face, it was not difficult to believe how Gano had won the favour of his teacher through sheer charm alone. Gano had had the same teacher for two years because he had not been able to graduate from the first grade and the teacher was content for she retained her charming helper. Gano's charisma made him a popular choice to lead church services, but his illiteracy was holding him back from being a leader respected for a biblical authority.

Challenged by Gano declaring himself hopelessly illiterate, a belief his wife also held, I determined to see what I could do. I started getting him to recognise the letters that made up his name, followed by other short and simple words; building on this until the whole alphabet was well covered with many examples. The start was laboriously slow. His main struggle was with his unbelief.

'Probably I am not able to read!' Gano would declare without emotion; his wife's laughter would ring out, not unkindly, but concluding nonetheless with a condemnatory, 'Probably!' But for as long as Gano did not give up, I was ready to spend literally hours every day to strive for a breakthrough. After our first nine-day stay in his house, Gano was reading very slowly – but reading. However, he was not able to understand what he read, such was his concentration to recognise the letters and pronounce the syllables. It took many months with Gano before he could read with understanding, but he succeeded through sheer determination. It would have been a much shorter time had we been able to stay a prolonged period in Manihala, but being itinerant did not allow us that luxury.

I enjoyed Gano's ways of going about his work. He kept pigeons, built coops for them with grass roofs, like miniatures of the people's own houses, raised up on really high stilts. He took delight in scattering corn on the ground and watching the pigeons take the seed. He could catch them with a cotton noose on the end of a bamboo which he could tighten from the other end when a pigeon stepped into the loop. He showered his birds by filling his mouth with water and spraying them under pressure through compressed lips yielding to the strain. I could joke with him, saying how glad I was to be his guest and not one of his pigeons and he would understand and laugh heartily, humour which other Buhid would not necessarily readily understand or appreciate.

He shared his life with us whenever we stayed in Manihala. On one visit Gano asked me whether I would like to go monkey hunting, not to eat, but to gain a pet. Wary about how far into the hills his traps were, I hesitated. He assured me they were close by, knowing how I struggled in the heat. My strength was just not what it once was, and I feared I would become a burden.

Gano and I were on foot following his eldest boy, 'Smail, who was riding their horse down the hill to the river way down below. Terribly hot, I was glad to arrive in the shadowy valley, cooling my feet in the running water, splashing it over my skin, burning with the sun and sweat. 'Smail came towards us, leading his horse for a drink at the edge of a banana grove, when a green pit viper suddenly reared up out of the undergrowth. I had not been aware of Gano's whereabouts, but he was on the scene in a couple of swift strides, with *fotol* drawn. Gano did not so much strike the highly venomous snake, but with the point of his *fotol*, thrust its head into the ground and with one continuous action, buried its head into the soft earth. The snake died instantly, not so much as even writhing in the usual death throes.

Gano put away his *fotol* into the hand-made wooden sheath tied by a cord about his waist. This whole action took only five seconds, from the moment he strode over to the time the pit viper was dead. He walked on, not so much as taking a second look at the snake, nor even making a comment about how near it had come to striking either 'Smail or the horse. Killing a snake was all in the course of a day's work. The equanimity he showed to what had taken place was similar to what I would have felt in squatting a mosquito. Even that is not a fair analogy for I would not have been able to contain a little triumphant cry of 'Got it!'

Gano stopped on the faint trail running close beside the river through the banana grove and looked back, beckoning me to follow. It had been a very short rest by the river and I encouraged myself to go on again, reasoning that the monkey traps were not far away and surely must be close by since we had already walked for the best part of an hour.

I stepped very gingerly through that undergrowth, through endless groves of banana palms imagining the many pit vipers concealed, together with all the other

Pausing on the trail
John Richards

nasties. I was very glad Gano was in front, seemingly walking with careless abandon. But I knew better than to think any Buhid was foolhardy, for they have the uncanny appearance of being quite off-guard. A lifetime of living in the jungle had made them acutely aware of their environment. So at one with the place, they noiselessly moved through the undergrowth, effortlessly walking along slippery trunks of fallen trees, wading through strong currents flowing at chest height without the slightest hesitation or false step. Near sheer slopes of hard-packed wet clay were negotiated without a moment's doubt. Such was the way Gano led me to the traps that I kept reminding myself were close by.

Now, more than an hour had passed and I dare say Gano could have made this journey in half that time had he not had me in tow, persuading him to choose the easier routes for my benefit that were not always the most direct ways. It was humbling to see his effortless progress, his bare brown shoulders hardly making any vertical movement as he glided over the uneven terrain. My body lurched this way and that in a most ungainly manner, now stooping, now leaping, whilst Gano serenely glided on before me. Ominously, 'Smail had stayed behind upriver with the horse and I began to wish I had done likewise.

I spirited myself on, very conscious of Gano's graciousness in putting up with my slow and cumbersome pace just to provide me with this rare treat and hopefully share the joy of seeing one of his elusive traps containing a monkey. Whenever I suggested that perhaps I could join some Buhid on one of their jaunts, they cautiously replied that it was a long way and I would probably get too tired. I was never very sure whether this was just social etiquette on their part to test how serious I was about joining them, or if this was their way of dissuading me from becoming a hindrance. Perhaps they were waiting for me to insist again and again to indicate my earnestness in joining them! Not wanting to be a nuisance, I never pursued as etiquette might have demanded. Gano was quite different though. Ready to accommodate my ways, the need for more rests and more to drink, he did not question such differences but calmly accepted them. He was genuinely pleased to have me with him, a feeling that was reciprocated.

The previous week he had caught two monkeys; one he kept at home on a long lead tied to a rope harness around the lower half of the monkey's body. He assured me that as soon as the monkey got accustomed to living with them, he would release it from its harness to roam freely about the house, but admitted that this could take up to six months. I was much taken by Gano's gentleness with the monkey, respectfully greeting it when coming home by placing his forehead against the forehead of the monkey and holding that greeting for a few seconds. Both monkey and Gano remained motionless with closed eyes, whilst Gano made low groans of satisfaction deep down in his throat. The other monkey he had caught had been sold to a Luktanon neighbour for more than five hundred pisos, equal to a Buhid's earnings in a week of trading the best quality bananas.

The jungle had by now become so dense that Gano led me to the river where we waded downstream, plunging suddenly into deep pools before stepping out again onto pebbly shallows. At least I was cooled by the water, having been drenched in sweat by this long trek down the valley. Continuing in this manner for the next quarter of an hour, Gano announced that we were close and had to leave the river at that point. Soaking my large handkerchief in the river and without wringing it out, I fastened it round my throbbing temples.

Gano climbed a steep clay bank with great agility and I followed with a great spurt of speed and a big bound that had me following hot on his tracks. I was foolish to really believe the traps were really quite that near! I don't know whether it was due to this untimely bravado of the older man past his prime and not yet having accepted the fact, but my lightning ascent of the bank, which surprised even me, now triggered Gano into a semi-sprint. He steamed on through the taller-than-man tropical grass, coarse and sharp to the skin, easily able to cut if grabbed, and was lost from sight. But there was the comfort of some kind of trail to follow, one which Gano had probably made himself on his successive trips made to the nearby traps.

The hill was steep and disturbingly went on up to a great height without the shade of a single tree. I had been warned that these tall grasslands in remote places – like the very spot where I now found myself alone – were the favoured habitats of pythons. I would be able to put up little resistance to a python now, should I have the misfortune to meet one.

Still Gano must be nearby.

I plodded on up the steep hillside, spotting the ground with great drops of sweat, which fell from my hands and brow as steadily as my pulse-rate. Toiling in that fashion for five minutes without stopping, I pushed myself on, not wanting to be left behind. My lungs ached so much that the hot air didn't seem to satisfy their craving for oxygen. I stopped and dizzily looked back down the hillside. Some 300 feet below, the river already looked distant, much of its course lost in the tangle of jungle. My headband no longer felt cool. I wished I had some water, for my throat was parched. I laboured on, coming to a junction in the trail, one going downhill to the river, the other leading on up to the nearing ridge. I wondered whether these monkey traps were across on the other side of the hill, for the ridge was probably only another 300 feet.

Taking the uphill trail, I struggled on, one heavy foot wearily following another, my head spinning with the effort, wondering whether I might faint if I were to keep that pace up for much longer. Still there was no sign of Gano. Perhaps he had taken the other trail at the junction, but I refused to reason that he would climb halfway up a hill and then drop down again to the river. I came around a corner to find Gano there smiling, waiting at another junction in the trail. This time the path ran left and right along the contour of the hill.

'The traps are very close now!' he greeted me with an indulgent smile. I was going to challenge him for misleading me about the closeness of these traps, but I did not have the breath to complain. Besides, his innocent expression made it difficult to accuse him of being devious. Upon reflection, no deceit was in him and I concluded that the words 'close by' was a relative term that had two totally different interpretations to Buhid and to foreigners unused to this environment.

Gano led at a gentle pace along the side of the hill, walking around a spur and into a slight defile running down the hillside from the very ridge top. We went towards this defile and I wondered about the difficulties of the way ahead, when Gano stopped in front of me, stooping down to an open trapdoor over a hole dug into the hillside. This was the first of his famous monkey traps. He had used sawn timber planks for the door, which was about one and a half feet in width as it was in length. The heavy door propped up by a flimsy-looking stick, had a vine attached to it. On the other end of the vine was tied a banana. Attracted by the banana, the monkey would enter into the hole, take hold of the banana which then would dislodge the stick supporting the open heavy door, and become trapped inside. Gano inspected the loose soil about the trap which determined that no monkey had been there that day. He invited me to go on and inspect the next trap. I told him to go on alone, to which he replied that it was 'nearby'. I do not understand why I trusted him, but I followed. True to his word this time the second trap was only a few paces away.

I noticed with excitement that the heavy door on this trap was shut and couldn't understand why Gano looked disappointed. His experienced eye though had taken it in at a glance, detecting a hole to the side of the trap's frame. The trapped monkey had dug itself out.

We returned home empty-handed. Apart from the first section of descent back down to the river, the way now was all uphill which I made such heavy going of that we didn't reach his house until sunset, much later than I expect Gano had anticipated. Gano never showed any impatience with me, perhaps applying that same belief in me as I had applied to bringing him to a literate level. I sat down on a log outside his house absolutely shattered, trying to convince myself that I was glad of the experience, a gratification that did not truly dawn for another few days after I had returned to the lowlands and its relative comforts. Only there could I reflect on these events with a growing fondness for my friend, admiration of Buhid ingenuity in devising such traps and glad of this rare glimpse a westerner could ever have of such things.

As I sat wasted outside Gano's house, another Buhid stopped his water buffalo on the trail running past. He came over without greeting, clutching a generous handful of small red fruit, like a small sweet pepper in shape, but more tapered, and placed these into my hands. I thanked him for these 'maculpa' and bit into its crunchy, bitter sweet flesh. Never had I enjoyed a maculpa as much as I savoured that one. I carried the remainder indoors to share with my hosts. Just as I came through the entrance, a hairy arm lunged down from above, stealing two maculpas from the small pile in my palms. Looking up, I saw Gano's pet monkey climbing away with the fruit, making threatening noises at me in case I had any ideas of retrieving what he now considered to be his own.

Mischievous as monkeys are, Gano's pet proved a liability.

'He has committed so many crimes!' confided Gano, months later, with a hint of despair. 'He has killed all but three of my pigeons and decapitated my favourite alimahon songbird. I cannot begin to tell you all the sins this monkey has committed, the food he has stolen, the utensils he has broken or damaged. The final straw was when I came home to find him with a lighter in his hand. Having adjusted the flame to full height, he just sat there repeatedly striking the flint, sending a huge flame up towards the cogon grass roof. Fearing that he would burn our house down, I sold him to a Luktanon!'

'How much did you sell him for?' I asked, amused by his audacity of making money out of a miscreant of a pet.

'Oh, the usual 500 pisos,' he replied, with a roguish grin. 'The fellow I sold him to is well pleased and as he keeps him outdoors I don't suppose much harm will occur!'

Before long, Gano had caught another monkey, this one proving to be a far less troublesome pet. However, Gano was perhaps more easily satisfied with this second monkey because like the Luktanon, he kept the pet out-of-doors.

Apart from the one-hour round trip to get washed and fetch drinking water, we looked forward to our visits to Manihala. Given the choice of a few days on the beach or a trip up to Manihala, our children opted for Manihala because of the horse riding. Gano so spoiled them, making a special saddle of braided vine that formed the frame across which he secured sacks for padding. Iain and Hannah loved riding down to the river and cantering across the gently sloping tops of the surrounding hills.

They had their falls and Gano showed just as much concern, if not more, for the well-being of our children as he did for his own. The whole community positively relished our children's visits. Once when Iain fell at full gallop, bareback, and hurt his arm quite badly, an older woman came over to check if it were broken. She showed much concern and offered to massage the injury, something they do especially in the case of a fracture, painfully knitting the bones back into place once again. Iain quickly assured her that his arm was feeling much better! Our children named Gano's horse 'Sheba' because they considered her a very regal animal, fit for carrying a queen. In truth, she was a stunted mare, ill-nourished on the meagre provision her grazing provided.

One Sunday afternoon, following the worship service and lunch, the church made a planned trip down the mountain to bathe in a pool at the foot of a waterfall. Quite a group of us went, leaving the village people-less except for the very old. Some of our party rode on horseback, others on water buffalo, but the majority went on foot, skipping jauntily, sweat streaming down faces and bare backs, everyone quickening their pace in anticipation of the cool deep waters running in the shade of cliff and bamboo.

The location lived up to its reputation. The waterfall came from quite a height, but instead of falling straight down into the pool below, it flowed down a steep gradient of rock, tumbling in waves of water along this natural flume, into a seemingly bottomless pool of green water. No one wasted a moment getting into the cool water, stripping down to just shorts, including all the women except for the unmarried ones who kept their T-shirts on. On one side rose a 15-foot cliff from which all the men jumped as the girls let out whooping cries and yelps to encourage their bravado. One of the men, pretending to be scared, clowned about on the edge of the cliff with knocking knees, much to the amusement of those below.

A diving board of two parallel tree limbs pointing upwards at 45 degrees, was fastened with vine to a tree growing on the edge of this cliff top, added a further ten feet to the descent. A twelve-year-old girl was the first to summon the courage to walk this precarious diving board and plummet off, putting all the males to shame. With nothing to hold onto once one had passed the supporting tree trunk, this feat required the most precise balance and head for heights to be able to walk upright; one had to sidle to the end of the branches at an angle. This was very difficult to do with wet feet.

A wonderful atmosphere, like that of being one big family, pervaded our pool. In truth they were all an extended family with in-laws, except for ourselves, but we were made to feel very much part of the group. One of the men, spotting a pit viper in a tree, shook the branch it was entwined around until eventually it fell into the pool below not so very far from where I was swimming. I was most relieved to see it swim in the opposite direction towards the water flume. The pit viper moved gracefully and swiftly through the water, its head and upper body craning clear of the water, looking all the while for a means of escape along the shore. Twice it unsuccessfully attempted to scale the sheer cliff face and came to a swift end with one well-aimed blow from a stick as soon as it mounted the rock beside the water flume.

When some Luktanon turned up, the Buhid women immediately put their tops on and our party did not stay much longer. Hannah enjoyed a cool ride back up to the summit of the hill on the back of a water buffalo, sharing this with two girls of similar age, with a fourth using the beast's tail to drag herself up.

'We're thinking of moving our village,' Bagaw, the patriarchal figure of the community, informed us. Not having turned fifty yet, he was one of the oldest people around with the exception of his ancient mother who rarely went out-of-doors these days. Bagaw had been trained at the Bible college. With his undisputed intelligence, considerable ability and charismatic character – recognised attributes that had him elected as the political representative for the Buhid in that area – he was without question the one in authority. It was rare for the Buhid to have such a leader, respected by all, in a society that otherwise had no hierarchical recognition.

'A plot of land has become available down the hill towards the road which will be much closer for our children to go to school,' explained Bagaw, informing us of a further prayer request before we closed our meeting in prayer. 'Another main consideration in buying this land will be the two springs that emerge within its boundaries!'

Living so far from good water had become a heavy burden on the community. At one time, the present site also had a spring, but after the earthquake of 1994, it had dried up, like many others had done, as the geological structures of the area were affected.

'There's one problem though – this new site is where we used to bury our dead! In the days when we used to chant to the spirits of the dead, during times of sickness for instance, we would implore the spirits to return to their resting place on this plot. In spite of the teaching that our Lord is superior in power to all these spirits put together, some are still wary and scared about moving onto a cemetery. Before such teaching not one of us would even have considered moving there!'

The Buhid had many fears and taboos, for most at one time or another had dabbled in the occult; some were steeped in potent witchcraft directed at either people or land. The demonic was very evident in accounting for certain deaths. Every place where a person had died became accursed in their reckoning, persuading them to abandon house and to move on a sufficient distance so as to be out of reach of the spirit of the dead. To ignore such taboos would result in the dead seizing one of the living to become a companion in the lonely nether world. Curses could be uttered by the living to bring about death by directly singling out an adversary, or indirectly by cursing a particular plot of land. These powers had become more developed owing to their being a non-confrontational people. Never using physical force, they sought revenge through the occult, a force they knew had insidious power except against a Christian walking in faith.

The occult became so developed that it functioned in many areas of their lives. If something was either lost or stolen, a medium was consulted, having the powers to know the whereabouts of the belonging, animal or person. Such a medium could even listen in on conversations from afar to know the plotting of an adversary.

Some practices related to unrequited love. If you wanted to cast an amorous spell on someone, you stole one of their flip-flops and whispered a spell over it – supposedly making the owner of the sandal fall in love with you. My wife lost a number of flip-flops! Rarely the whole pair would go missing, as this would have been simply attributed to someone going off with them by mistake or as an act of theft; but frequently just one of a pair went missing. No one ever took one of my flip-flops! Alexandra and I made it a daily habit to break, through prayer, any curse or spell placed upon us.

'You know,' I mused aloud in reply to Bagaw's concern of building upon the cemetery, 'it probably isn't just a coincidence this cemetery site being available just now, when you as a church are grasping the freedom from demonic interference. God is putting this test before you. If you stand in faith and put to the test this belief, then you will stand!'

By the time of our next visit three months later, the cemetery had been purchased and building was underway. Although there were initial reports of supernatural goings-on, the strong prayed with the weak, Gano taking a prominent role, standing on the promises of Scripture

> Submit yourselves, then, to God. Resist the devil, and he will flee from you. (Jas. 4:7, NIV)

The church dedicated the land to be a safe dwelling-place, with a number of us praying very specifically about the binding of demonic forces. We were curious to hear some time later from lowlanders living at the base of the Manihala hill region: they described seeing handcuffed demonic beings.

During the first visits to Manihala, we were put up in a different household each time, a fine way to get acquainted with a family. The patriarchal Bagaw would assign us to a certain family. This was never easy for us or our hosts since the matter never seemed to be discussed in advance. The family had little choice, without appearing totally rude and inhospitable. Whatever our hosts may have felt, suddenly being made responsible for our needs for the next nine days, they were nevertheless exceptionally gracious. Our ways amused them – like the sewn-up sheets we had made into sleeping bags, or the combing of my beard, the cleaning of a pan until shiny with a pan scourer, the knocking of our heads on the low roof beams or door lintels or the joking banter between husband and wife. We detected on their part a sense of relief on discovering we could enjoy a good laugh too.

Meal times could be hilarious in a Buhid home. With plates set out on the floor, dogs would gravitate, looking hopefully for a dropped morsel but never given any encouragement. Hogday kept a couple of dogs, tolerated at times to come in to the home. The dogs knew they were not supposed to be there at meal times, but Hogday was too preoccupied talking with us to notice the sly pets slinking in almost on their bellies along the wall behind us in the semi-gloom of the interior, lit by two guttering paraffin cans. The dogs positioned themselves in the shadows as close as they could to the food, ready to make a pounce should anything fall from our fingers. Hogday would suddenly break off in mid-sentence and, with loud and fretful exclamations that set his stammer off, would send the dogs slinking back into the shadows. Meanwhile the chickens were having a fine feed underneath the house, particularly just below where the youngest of the children sat with a hand encrusted in grains of rice that, not very expertly, fed a mouth likewise encrusted. A good amount fell between the slats – as was true in our case initially, before we better mastered the art of eating rice with our fingers.

One time we arrived late in Manihala because Gano had had to wait for the banana dealer to pay him for the several hundred bananas he had brought her that morning. She promised to pay by midday, then it was 'in just a little while' which became 'later' said in a tone that expressed annoyance that Gano just did not give up and go home without a piso. He had waited till late afternoon when the dealer then said 'next week' and so we went home with him, arriving at the village at dusk. We were about to take our shoes off at his door when he cleared his throat to get our attention.

'*Faduwasay* – this is yours!' he simply said. We looked up to see him disappear around the corner of his house. I followed him with one shoe on and the other one off.

'When I heard of your visit and that your children were with you, I hurried to get this finished in these last few days!'

I was flabbergasted for it was a complete house. He had given no indication of even considering building us a home. I was literally speechless for a few moments. I called Alexandra and the children and we all stood outside, trying to convey our appreciation of so generous a gift. Meanwhile, Gano had untied the knot made in the rattan fastening between the sliding door and frame and lit an oil lamp tin strategically placed by the door, all ready for our visit. The light poorly illuminated an interior made of bark walls – long broad sections of bark forming vertically hung panels secured to a bamboo frame with more rattan. The roof was beautifully made of cogon thatch laid so straight that it appeared combed, clamped by bamboo slats, tied to the straightest branches ever seen that formed the roof rafters.

When the next morning dawned, we slid open a large window-screen that looked down on the village, erected in a natural amphitheatre below, the simple chapel built in the centre. The smoke of the wood fires cooking breakfast issued through the thatch of almost every roof as though steaming in the sun. The sun having only just appeared over the margin of the distant sea, gilded the edge of a mother-of-pearl cloud mass. Tracts of sea were bright with morning light whilst the many islands were etched in scintillating silhouette. The softness of dawn soon vanished like a spell losing its potency. We braced ourselves for the earnest harshness of the tropical sun.

We had always admired this view of the South China Seas breaking on the shore and the stretches of coral reefs. Like a patchwork quilt, the paddy fields stretched out from the base of the hills. Depending on the season, from this height they either mirrored the sky or, with an emerald green lustre, stretched like a perfect lawn. Groves of banana covering the nearby hill horizon; some lazily stretching delicate fronds which shimmied in the breeze, seemed to be keeping time with the sawing of the cicadas. Other fronds made ragged by the wind, fluttered like bunting against the lovely sky. Lines of coconut palms marked the margin of the island. Set against a backdrop of sandy beach and sparkling sea, those palms were also moved by the warm winds that curled the waves.

'Gano built it all by himself,' Bagaw, Gano's father-in-law, informed us, proud of this generous gesture. 'It was Gano's idea as well and we all thought it a good one!'

After the evening meal was cleared away (which Gano and Deborah still insisted on providing, to help maximise our time spent teaching and visiting), Hannah and Iain began to form hand shadows on the inside wall of the house. Gano and Deborah were at first surprised by the simple ingenuity required, as well as the imagination to make dog and snake shapes. Their youngest one began to cry, cowering at his mother's side, finding the gigantic snake's head looming threateningly down upon us, all too dramatic. His parent's explanation and laughter eventually pacified him.

Gano fashioned his hands to create a dog's head and with evident delight, finally succeeded. He announced to his children, '*Ido!*' – their word for dog – making the mouth open and close. Deborah, giggling much, abandoned her youngest child to come over to where the poor paraffin light flickered from the top of an old tin. She made a snake appear, elegantly ascending the wall. '*Abiyanon!*' she declared, laughing with childlike delight. Husband and wife proceeded to act out a drama, *ido* attacking *abiyanon* and vice-versa. Still unconvinced that this was at all entertaining, their youngest pouted his lower lip.

We retired to our house next door and spent a quarter of an hour laying out our bedding and hanging our mosquito nets. As soon as we were quiet, we heard

Deborah's voice pierce the still night with the exclamation of *'abiyanon!'* proceeded by Gano retorting with *'ido'*, the giggling exchange continuing for a good five minutes. We were surprised at how evidently novel shadow plays were to the Buhid, especially considering them to be such a playful people, not lacking either in practical inventiveness.

What a complete surprise this house had been! Its construction spoke not only of a generous spirit, but of a welcome; an invitation to be part of their community. This was a rare privilege knowing how the Buhid, with the exception of Batangan, did not permit outsiders to be part of their communities. This hut in Manihala was soon followed by a second one at Apnagan at the other end of this hill ridge, again unsolicited and unexpected.

In the flow
John Richards

Chapter Eleven:

On Muddy Hill

It was at the time of the evening meeting when the fire was noticed. As some of the Christians in Apnagan were gathering to continue with the introductory course to the Mangyan Bible School, the latecomers had detected a fiery glow and a faint plume of smoke rising just behind the nearby summit.

'Sagyom – Sagyom, you had better come! Look!' said one excited young man, knowing Sagyom's house to be in the near vicinity of the fire. Sagyom came quickly from the front of the church where he had been preparing to teach. He and everyone else went running towards the fire. Sagyom's house was indeed on fire.

Noticing a pile of sawn timber under the burning house, Ihit – a strong and determined-looking Buhid – wrapping an extra shirt about his head to protect his hair, went towards the blaze. Able to endure the intense heat like no one else, Ihit salvaged several specially sawn pieces, carefully stacked under the house for the building of a new house. The timber was not only costly, but the product of felling, dragging tree trunks all the way down to the sawmill in the lowlands before carrying the sawn sections back uphill again.

Sagyom and Lionayan were relieved to see their three children appear at the scene. The fire was too advanced to do anything with, other than watch it burn itself out. There followed much questioning to determine how the fire had started. Their three children had left the house

176

Sagyom and his family
John Richards

shortly after their parents had gone to church; the cooking fire had been put out as too had all the lamps. It was all something of a mystery. Sagyom had built his home almost on the very top of the hill, sensitive to the beauty of the view all around from that summit elevation. Therefore sparks from a neighbour's fire (sometimes a cause of house fires) could not have reached Sagyom's home and kindled the thatch. Not long passed before someone attributed the fire to an act of sabotage by the neighbouring Luktanon community who allegedly carried out intimidating acts to spirit the Buhid off their land, like repeatedly vandalising the Buhid water pump.

The blaze had been so hot that even the metal cooking pots had melted in the fire. Losing everything, they literally only had the shirts on their backs and the Bibles in their hands. The community rallied around, providing them with clothes, many quite new, and more domestic utensils than they had ever owned before. Gaynop arranged a team of men to help Sagyom put up a new house in a matter of about four or five days. We replaced his small library of books and OMF, recognising his acts of service to the church, made a financial gift. We discovered later that this gift covered the amount of money hidden in the roof thatch.

What was possibly meant to harm Sagyom and the community only resulted in the family feeling loved and cared for and if anything, left them not much worse off than they were before. It demonstrated what a close-knit community they were, bound not only by kindred blood ties but also by bonds of Christian brotherhood.

Sagyom never once failed to be in the party who met us at the start of the trail to Muddy Hill as we referred to Apnagan. He would greet us by taking a pace or two towards us with an almost apologetic air, feeling perhaps conspicuous meeting the *Amerikanos*. His good-humoured grin was accentuated by an imperial beard he was able to grow and wear to good effect; most Filipinos do not have much facial hair beyond the upper lip area. His eyes shone with a lucid brilliance that testified to a man without deceit or pretension. The warm greeting was most infectious. No matter how wearisome the journey had been, Sagyom's smile was so engaging that you had to smile back.

We have often been asked what we did for friendships, being isolated from the rest of the OMF team. Much as we appreciated our international team members, we would have undoubtedly felt very lonely were it not for special Buhid friends like Sagyom. I think we were also fortunate in having a number of western missionaries who paved the way for us, so that the remnant of our western ways was not new to many Buhid. Aside of this rationale, a distinct bond was fashioned early on, God-given I believe, because certain friendships and trust just flourished and matured to such a level that we could safely confide in each other, feel a burden shared and have a concern prayed for.

'*Faduwasay* –' Sagyom politely interjected, as I took hold of the straps of my backpack. Having already premeditated this move of carrying my pack, he came forward to take up the heaviest of all our cargo. Gone were my independent days when I declined such help, when I liked to make it to the top of the hill under my own steam carrying my own belongings. I had been embarrassed at first by the Buhid's assistance, making me feel the white master lording it over native servants. But now having at least a couple of extra boxes of medicines and literature, I was glad of this help. They too were glad to be able to express their appreciation of our visits and were embarrassed should we insist on carrying our own bags.

Sagyom had the ability to listen very carefully, keen to understand a question or a point before answering or commenting. He had the habit of asking questions to confirm his understanding before venturing an opinion, although there was nothing tedious in his doing this since he was not circuitous but came to the point. His answers were always valued for he spoke the truth in love, preferring not to follow the custom of answering by inferring or by innuendo. For this reason he made an able pastor, ready to get alongside others in difficulties, always chosen in connection with delicate issues.

An excellent teacher, Sagyom very thoroughly communicated the truth, always faithful to the spirit of the message, confessing ignorance at times rather than offering a possibly flawed opinion, which might be mistaken for gospel truth. His teaching was always well thought out and clearly presented, an admirable quality rare in a culture that did not have a literary or academic tradition. Raised in a different society, Sagyom could have been a doctor or a lawyer, having the ability to retain information, analyse it and make a judgement.

For two consecutive years, the Philippines had the La Nina phenomena – rain throughout dry season making the mud very bad. The Buhid walked with care but sure-footedly, whereas we danced along beside them with flailing arms at times and bodies helplessly lurching this way and that, much to the amusement of the children and the concern of the adults. Our feet just did not seem to be made the same way as theirs. Buhid toes are beautifully spaced and splayed, never having been deformed within shoes, and so are agile, subtle to grip the hillside, gaining a purchase in places we could not tread.

'You know, people pay a fortune back in our country to have mud treatments to beautify their skin,' remarked my wife, gingerly picking her way through the fetlock-deep mud. 'You Buhid must have the most beautiful feet in the world!'

Gaynop was walking ahead to show where to put her feet and being the gentlemen that he was, sometimes offered her a hand over gaps that had to be jumped. He stopped to look at his foot, raised out of the mud. With a cursory glance at our misshapen toes, Gaynop nodded thoughtfully before declaring, 'Yes, that's true!' He walked on with serious demeanour leaving us exchanging amused glances.

Alexandra did not trust my help in the same manner as she placed her total faith in Gaynop's guidance. It spared me from the recriminations should I have chosen the less desirable passage through the quagmire that might possibly result in a slip into a deep water buffalo mud pool. Men like Gaynop went to great lengths to find alternative routes. He would even unsheath his *fotol* to carve out footholds in the clay of a steep slope.

'Would you like me to cut you a staff?' suggested Gaynop to Alexandra.

'What would I be doing with a staff? I have enough trouble managing on two legs, so a third one will only make it harder and get in the way!'

Gaynop thought this very funny and had us all chuckling because of his infectious bronchial wheeze of a laugh.

'It would be easier with a staff, an extra point of contact with the ground to help keep your balance,' I said.

'I can't be doing with it!'

As her husband I knew the tone well and knew to back off when hearing it. A little further on, Gaynop cut her a staff nonetheless which Alexandra reluctantly accepted.

'Oh, this staff makes a big difference!' was my wife's verdict in less than a minute.

'Thank you, Gaynop!' I thought to myself, envious of how he succeeded in areas where I never could.

Two hours on the trail with a couple of stops brought us to Muddy Hill, arriving at the hut Waydinan had built us, next to his own.

Into his sixties, Waydinan and his wife – Ignay – had been long-time missionaries across the island at Datag Bonglay, with Monay and Sagyom, and were therefore in wholehearted accord with our purpose and graciously went out of their way to make our life in Apnagan as easy as possible. Gallons of water appeared just when I was thinking of getting some, piles of wood were left when stocks had diminished, an oil lamp brought near dusk on the first night if we had just returned from visiting others. Cooked rice and sometimes a dish of vegetable stew would be quietly left just inside the door. Other Buhid performed such kindnesses too, but Waydinan and Ignay did the lion's share. Waydinan had even thoughtfully constructed the raised kitchen hearth at a level convenient to our height.

Waydinan related a specific time when they, together with the elders, prayed for a missionary family to be sent to their tribe. The remarkable thing is that they prayed in September of 1993, the month of our momentous field trip passed at the Bible school and that impressionable trip up the misty mountain at dawn to Ayan Bekeg. The Buhid did not know God had answered their prayer that very same month by impressing upon us the needs of the tribal churches and giving us a special love for the Mangyan. Nor did we know back then that the Buhid had prayed for a family. Both the Buhid and ourselves were aware of a deep need that kept both parties searching the Lord in prayer. How perfectly God brought the two of us together, characterised by that special empathy we had towards one another from the very outset.

It could rain heavily for days on end, and moving about on those clay hill ridges was very taxing. When conditions were at their worst, we only ventured out when we had to, to visit the sick and needy and run sessions in the church. The call of nature would be put off time and again until you could no longer possibly ignore it. Not only did you get soaked in the process since you had to move inordinately slowly in the treacherous conditions, but you arrived back at your door caked to the top of the calves with sticky clay. This involved using a fair amount of water to remove it, to avoid soiling the mud-free zone within the hut. The more you went out and used up the water, meant the sooner you had to fetch more water. Mindful of the problem it was for us, the Buhid would have been happy to provide all our water needs, which they often did, but we had that dogged determination to do what we could and not become totally inept. We balked at the idea that we regarded them as lackeys.

From the first night, we gathered in the chapel standing on the very ridge top, calling all the folk by striking the iron girder section hung from an eave of the church. It would be about 7.30 when the majority congregated, having just cleared away their evening meal. I was often asked questions about the world beyond them, other nations they assumed I was part of, crediting me with such an encyclopaedic knowledge that I was bound to frequently disappoint them.

'*Faduwasay* – tell us who this Saddam Hussein is? Why are the *Amerikanos* bombing his country?' As best and as impartially as I could, I explained the colonial and post-colonial history of the Middle East leading up to the conflicts daily reported on the radio. The Buhid had such a natural curiosity that had only emerged with their first trusting the missionaries. Before that time, and indeed still today, among villages unreached by missionaries and other outsiders, the Buhid are deeply suspicious of anyone and anything beyond their immediate ken, never inquiring lest it bring trouble and incurred the wrath of the vengeful, ancestral spirits.

'So where is Iraq – is it a country mentioned in the Bible?'

The Bible was their one source of reference to world affairs, other than the radio. Similarly they wanted to know about all the other protagonists mentioned in the report dealing with Iraq and why they were behaving in the way they were.

Concept of time was hard to grasp. With no recorded history of their own, they did have an oral tradition going back to the time of Moro invasions of the west coast of Mindoro, but even this they were unable to place in the context of time.

'We Buhid – that is to say our forefathers – once fought a battle with the Moros, into the hills near Datag Bonglay,' began Duday, one of the older men who often adopted the role of oral chronicler of tribal history. The Moros were marauding Muslim seafarers from the southern island of Mindanao, taking control of the whole Philippine archipelago just prior to the Spanish claim and rapid conquest of the islands. 'There is a pile of stones marking where the battle was fought. The Moros had long *fotols*, very ferocious and bloodthirsty men they were. We Buhid do not like to fight but were eventually provoked to defend our people and lands. It is said that many bamboo spear traps were set along the trails to kill or maim the Moros! Anyway, a battle was fought. We don't know any longer who won, but the Moros didn't come back again!'

'If that were the case, then I suppose you could say the Buhid won,' I remarked to the old man.

'That I don't know – we don't like to fight,' the old one replied, his eyes shining with much good humour, but avoiding any glimpse of pride in the possible victory of his people.

They were seemingly unaffected by the 333 years of Spanish colonialisation, although the tribe to the south – the Hanunoo – welcomed the survivors of a Spanish galleon shipwrecked on the southern reefs. These Spaniards married Hanunoo women and spent the remainder of their lives with the tribe. To this day, certain Hanunoo bear Spanish features such as a prominent nose, and the full beards that some men are able to grow. The 48 years of American occupation passed by unnoticed by the Buhid, until the Japanese invaded.

Occasional sorties were made by the Japanese into the Mindoro hills searching for Filipino soldiers fighting a guerrilla war, killing a few Mangyan, roasting their bodies on a spit to fill their fellows with horror. That is the sum total of Buhid Mangyan history so the concept of a long-detailed change of rulers and powers vying for control over vast territories, bringing cultural changes, demands much imagination on their part.

'Are the Romans still living in Israel?' was a question among others that highlighted the need for further history lessons to try to satisfy some of their great curiosity about the world beyond Mindoro. This I did as best I could with no resources to hand. I drew time lines on the chalkboard, on which I plotted their known history. Plotting biblical events with an appropriate gap on the line to give some perspective to time back through the centuries beyond the time of their known history aroused true amazement, greeted by much clicking of tongues, scratching of heads and even little whoops of incredulity.

Geography lessons were required concurrently. Before they could understand the concept of a map, their village had first to be plotted on a map. Changing the scale, their home was next drawn in relation to other Buhid villages, marking the rivers, mountains and roads. In this manner, the scale was further reduced to show the whole island, then the Philippine archipelago. With a blow-up globe, we were able to show Scotland, and transposed kilometres into a more familiar measurement – the distance a Buhid could walk in a day, estimating that it would take the best part of two years to walk to Scotland! The Buhid were utterly astonished by the size of the world, putting their previously considered large island into diminutive proportion – a fact they greeted with more tongue clicking, shaking of heads and incredulous interchanges with their neighbours.

Only then did the maps in the back of the Bible begin to make sense. Before then they were nothing more than incomprehensible squiggles and esoteric symbols. At least my interest in history assisted in giving some historical structure upon which they could place this information. I was far more taxed trying to explain how a voice can come out of a radio box or how moving images can be projected around the world in an instant by satellite!

The Buhid struck me as people full of wonder at the world around them, intrigued, for instance, by how an aeroplane appears to scratch the blue from the sky's dome and how that dome is capable of healing itself once more.

One morning, after the teaching session in the Apnagan Church, I produced several photographs of Jerusalem to give some idea of the appearance of the city. They crowded round with much clicking of tongues, impressed by the size and beauty of the place, with many questions about why the houses had flat roofs, and other such differences they noted from the world they knew.

'Faduwasay – do you mean to say there really is a city called Jerusalem?' Dado was a young man on the fringe of the church. He had the most searching expression on his face after my affirmative reply and went on to ask, 'So there is a real country called Israel? And what about Egypt?' His animation grew upon every positive response. Then he came to his life-changing conclusion, 'So Jesus Christ is a real person?'

Dado had already been baptised, following the example of all the others in a village where 49 out of the 50 households were believers, and yet he had thought the Bible was all fictional, a great collection of interesting adventures with plenty of moral teaching and applications. Not only were the Bible stories exciting to read and the church fellowship warm but being a

Christian in that environment gave one a real sense of belonging. It was seemingly for these reasons that Dado had professed faith in Christ and had been baptised.

In churches where scriptural knowledge was poor, where inadequate teaching abounded, such a non-believer was more plausible. Knowing that he followed the truth and not a fable transformed Dado. From then on he was at all the meetings.

One of the elders remarked, 'Dado is the fastest growing Christian in the village.' Sagyom had seen him hitching up his mud sledge to his water buffalo one Sunday morning and asked why he was not going to church.

'But I am going to church,' Dado had insisted. 'I am going to get Onan!' Dado sent an impish smile towards Sagyom who had suspected him of preferring to work on the Lord's Day rather than to worship God. An elderly believer, Onan was almost crippled with arthritis and no longer able to climb the hill to church. Although well cared for by his wife and neighbouring grown-up children, no one had thought of getting him to church. Dado saw to that practical detail from that time on, leading his water buffalo up the steep hill with the elderly Onan smiling coyly, leaning back against the side of the sledge, his chin resting on his tucked-up knees.

Dado came to our house after the meetings to ask questions about the Bible, often with long pauses to take it all in. One day he came to buy a Buhid New Testament. He told me that he had been putting five pisos aside for the last seven weeks from the money received from selling bananas in order to save enough to buy a copy. I was curious to know why he wanted to buy another one since he already had one still in good condition.

'This one is for my mother who lives way up the Siyangi River. She does not know the truth. Since I am not often there and there being no other Christians in her village, she will need to read God's words to know him.'

How the church would grow dynamically if there were more Dados, with his natural concern for others expressed in sacrificial ways. However, in one thing Dado was not exemplary. His wife brought a complaint to the church elders one day.

'Since Dado has started to attend all these meetings, he now spends all his time with his head buried in the Bible. If one of our children cries he complains and expects me to stop cooking to attend to the child whilst he goes on reading!' She tossed her head impatiently, pushing her long dishevelled hair back with a hand. 'From now on I am not coming to church!' she petulantly declared. 'I am angry with the God who has made Dado useless!'

The elders deliberated for a while and, scratching their heads, said there was nothing they could do since what Dado was doing, the reading of the Bible, was a good thing; so how could they admonish him for that?

The matter was eventually brought to my attention and Dado was none too pleased when I took issue with him about his behaviour. I informed him that God had given him a wife and children and it was his duty to love them. How was he showing love by ignoring them?

'But that is not what you preached last Sunday!' Dado retorted. 'You pointed out that God told Joshua to meditate on God's Word day and night. That is exactly what I am doing!'

He acquiesced before long, after being shown the scriptures instructing husbands to love their wives. His wife did not complain again and judging by her reappearance at church, she had overcome her jealousy of God.

Chapter Twelve:

Finding Peace in Death

Alexandra received word of a Buhid neighbour being admitted to hospital. He only had a gall bladder problem and had waited two weeks, before being told that an operation was required at a different hospital. Surgery was regarded by many as the last resort because the success rate was not high, a statistic not helped by patients who, hoping for a natural recovery and not gaining it, had left it too late for much surgical success.

Unfortunately the delays continued at the other hospital. He was made to fast several times in preparation for theatre, only for the operation to be cancelled at the last minute. This considerably aggravated his stomach ulcer. He had waited and suffered quite long enough, so we decided to intervene. An existing relationship between the hospital and our mission through some funding provided some hope of starting the procedure moving. These modest funds allowed tribal folk to be given a bed for the first time and not be told to make do with lying on a part of the corridor floor. As so much depends on relationships in Asia, we felt a reasonable confidence in having something done for our neighbour.

The doctor in charge seemed knowledgeable about our friend's case. As we had not met with this doctor before, we passed some time responding to his many questions about our work with the tribes. The interview seemed to have gone well; our credibility was established, which was all-important within the Asian context and favourable to seeing appropriate action taken. During the course of the conversation, the doctor recounted his experience of a medical mission to the 'minorities' – a Luktanon euphemism referring to the tribes. The NPA had turned up demanding treatment and medicines as well. He asked us about the peace and order situation in our part of the island and whether we encountered many NPA ourselves. We were frequently asked this question in the lowlands; we answered vaguely, so as not to compromise our neutrality and possibly jeopardise our purpose in being there.

The next day's operation was cancelled again, requiring our neighbour to fast for yet another day. That night he vomited blood. Earlier his faeces had been black too, signifying that his ulcer was bleeding.

At first our patient had been quite closed to talking about spiritual matters, but as life's uncertainties mounted, he became open to being prayed for and agreed to pass the time by having John's Gospel read to him in parts by Alexandra. He began to share how he had been a church-goer and with his wife had even attended, for a brief time, a Bible school in Manila – a training course, sponsored by the Koreans. He admitted that their main reason for going to Manila was for the adventure, to go beyond the island and sample life in the capital. With all travel expenses paid and full board and lodging provided, it was an offer too good to miss, having the appeal of a holiday for a couple who had had to work hard in the hills all their lives in order to find their next meal. Who could blame them for their unspiritual motivation? However, they did not seem to profit much from the teaching; they soon became disenchanted with the church on their return home and ceased attending the meetings.

As the Bible was read, the sick man began to nod his head in agreement. At times, the abdominal pain became so great that he began to shiver, sometimes shaking as he clasped his arms about his knees drawn up into his chest.

'Perhaps I should stop reading now,' suggested Alexandra, placing the open book down on her lap.

'No!' the patient replied through clenched teeth. 'Read on!'

The pain was not always so bad and at times he seemed able not to let it interfere with his interacting with those about his bedside. The Word of God had a profound effect on him and during those times when not doubled up with pain, he would exclaim with conviction, 'That's true' and pressed Alexandra, who was wary about overtiring him, to read on. He warmed to our praying as he transferred his hope from the doctor to the Lord and took us into his confidence.

'I have been wandering all my life, dabbling in this and that, trying to find reason and purpose to my life. When I had finished with the Koreans, I lost interest in a church that did not seem to give much of a message. Maybe I just could not understand back then what it was they were teaching.

'I have seen much injustice, the rich oppressing the poor, those with the gun taking away land from the poor and defenceless, even murdering for the sake of gaining a few hectares! I have grown weary and sick of seeing those who are supposed to uphold justice do nothing or worse still, back those who perpetrate the crimes. So many are twisted; their ways are not straight, but devious routes through the jungle, promising to go in one direction – but no sooner have you gone a little way along the trail when you soon discover their way doubles back on itself and heads in the opposite direction.'

The patient had fine dark brows which for much of the time were furrowed as he relived the anxieties and disappointments, the regrets in his life. His whole person exuded frustration. His powerful limbs, still strong in spite of the fasting, the illness and all the lying about in hospital, looked as though they could still assert his will. His bearing was a noble one. He was of the tribe to the south, who in their own language called themselves the Hanunoo, meaning 'the true', regarding themselves as the true Mangyan. Not ashamed of being a minority they held their heads high, proudly wore the loincloth long after many of the other Mangyan (besides those from the interior) gave up wearing it for the derision it caused in the lowlands.

A softening became detectable in his eyes; they were no longer expressing the defiance we had always known. The haughty look of the one who always stood on the nearside shelf at the back of the jeepney, no matter who was standing there before, was fading. He had always struck a revolutionary image with his longer-than-usual hair, often secured by a rolled up bandanna of red or white, reminiscent of Che Guevara.

'Even with the NPA I grew tired and disillusioned. Theirs is a lust for power at any cost that sometimes drives them more than their desire to see justice done. It's true that man is corrupt as the Bible says we are – no one is right, truly all have gone astray, some more than others. I have wanted to do what is right – I have not chased after riches, I have not thrown in my lot with swindlers to flaunt my success and lord it over my fellow man. In the end, tired with all the ways of the world, I have sought to mind my own business; I moved house last year to just next to you but I had not found peace. I have my enemies. I wanted to start anew but have been prevented by the past catching up with me.

In fact I had decided it's impossible to start afresh, that is until you began to read the teachings of Christ. Here there is hope. Read me some more!'

That night the patient lost so much blood vomiting and through his bowels that he needed a transfusion. The operation was postponed again, this time because he was too weak to assure his surviving the ordeal. More blood was needed during the day. With no blood bank held at the hospital, the procedure entailed searching out the hospital porter to negotiate a deal to find one of his many contacts who had the blood group required. With a typhoon blowing through for the past two days and now with storm signal two being declared for Oriental Mindoro, the price of blood had doubled! Storm signal two closed schools and businesses to keep people off the streets as they might be injured, even killed by flying debris in the air, or by trees or large branches coming down, or by floods causing landslides. Therefore to go out and search for someone with that blood group could be dangerous – at least that was the rationale. However, the weather was not particularly threatening at that hour, and had not deterred us from walking the mile over the hill to come to the hospital that morning.

Our patient was in considerable pain as we gathered round him to pray. The outlook looked particularly bleak with no more medical hope (if there ever had been, with what now became clear as intentional neglect of this ex-NPA individual). Only the Lord could preserve our friend now. Before we started to pray though, the patient exclaimed, 'You know, whether I live or die, I am in God's hands!'

He wanted to say more but pain prevented him. Beginning to pray, his rebellious teenage son made a point of standing close by us at that moment of intercession, sensing prayer was the remaining hope for his father. The son had been sent for and had arrived promptly the previous day, shocked to find his father in such a state. No sentimentality was evident in their meeting; the father maintained a strict demeanour with a son wise to all the tricks to shirk his duties. The son kept a certain distance to avoid the reproach of his father's tongue.

Having prayed, the father asked to have more of John's Gospel read. As Alexandra read, his brow was no longer furrowed. Still he interjected with the occasional 'That's true' and when physically unable to speak, he nodded his head in a very determined fashion to indicate his assent.

'There are no lords like Jesus,' declared the weakened man. 'He speaks what is true. His leading is the only one worth following.' He closed his eyes, feeling the need to rest. His wife cast us a worried look, for her man, normally so strong and assertive, was decidedly declining and death seemed quite probable – and yet, at the same time, inconceivable. Alexandra closed the Bible and thought about taking the fresher air outside the dirty ward that smelt so much of sickness, decay and drains. There wasn't the slightest hint of disinfectant.

'Read some more!' groaned the patient. 'You know I am his and he is with me. The fight I've fought all my life is over, I have found meaning and peace!'

Alexandra reopened her Bible and gladly read on. Meanwhile I spoke with the teenage son outside suggesting that he make peace with his father and ask his forgiveness for anything he might need to put right with him. The son looked awkward, and made no reply. When I went back into the ward again, the son followed me and we stood together by the father's bedside. Looking up, the weary man smiled faintly at his son, standing there unable to utter a word. I encouraged the lad, in a quiet voice, to say something. With a clarity that imminent death can sometimes give, and no longer caring for pretence, the father sensed what we were about and smiled more broadly now, raising a hand towards his firstborn son. He nodded his head and magnanimously said: 'There's nothing to forgive!' before there was any utterance of repentance.

The next morning, our new brother in the faith had passed on before us, beyond all the suffering and intrigue, the lies and corruption. The battle had been won. Sure of where he was going, death held no fear. Now he was with the army of the Lord, with the One who will uphold justice, call to account even those who escaped justice in this world and judge with righteousness. He was set apart in the new kingdom that will know no pain, a kingdom characterised by true holiness.

'We can operate now,' said the doctor emerging from nowhere. The wife looked at us, puzzled. We asked the doctor to explain himself.

'We can carry out a post-mortem and verify the cause of death. It will prove useful to a couple of medical students who happen to be here this morning!'

'No!' exclaimed the widow with a look of horror and absolute disdain flashing momentarily from her face. Turning her back on the doctor she signified that the matter was closed. He merely shrugged his shoulders and disappeared again.

A health co-ordinator from the Mangyan Tribal Church Association later came to report that he had succeeded in finding a grave lot. The municipal cemetery refused to have any more Mangyan buried within their site and it had been hard to persuade the warden of the Chinese cemetery to allow the burial of one from the minorities. More than was proper was asked for, and, out of desperation, the money exchanged hands.

The typhoon was blowing and squalls of rain lashed down from a grey storm-tossed sky as we carried the corpse in a rattan mat across the wastes of the cemetery to the waterlogged corner where a grave plot had been allocated. The corpse still looked muscular and noble in death. We were four men who began to dig the grave with picks and shovels. The soil was like waterlogged bread dough clinging to shovels, hands and bare feet. The teenage son set to with something of the energy and determination that his father was noted for, relieved to be doing something physical for once after all the impotent waiting about the hospital corridors and lingering by the bedside with the dawning inevitability of the coming end. The deeper the grave went, the greater became the problem with the water. We worked furiously in an attempt to beat the flood, but no sooner had we laid the corpse in the grave than the muddy waters rose and covered him. Only a loose corner of the matting floated on the surface a moment or two longer.

The widow lowered down a basket filled with a thermos flask, a towel and some other items of clothing and utensils. The grave warden watched the basket as it made a splash in the grave pool below. Something horrendous glinted in his greedy eye as he asked what was in the basket. I shuddered to think what he might do once our party was gone – a thought that struck Alexandra as well at the time. We were also concerned, for other reasons, about why this basket was placed with the dead but knew this was not the occasion to deal with it. We were burying one who died in certain hope of being with the Lord and no longer required the articles of this passing world.

Our Mangyan brethren felt a sense of despair – the intrigue at the hospital, the refusal of burial rights at the municipal cemetery, this waterlogged plot, the gloom of the typhoon blowing for a fourth day – even the influence of the foreigner which had been of no avail with the doctor. One of them looked wistfully at a tiered rank of concrete sarcophagi and asked the warden what the purchase price for one of these would be. Certainly it would be beyond the means of the poor, keeping them from any dignity even in death.

'Some may look to the concrete tombs across the way there,' I began the graveside address to the bleak gathering of the rain-swept, mud-splattered few, 'and think of the dignity that the dead are buried with there. But our brother here laid in the muddy water is better off by far than the richest and most revered of the land who have died unprepared to meet their Maker and Judge. Their funerals may have been grand, many may have mourned the passing with even the most influential turning out, but what is that compared to our brother who is now welcomed into heavenly mansions in the great company of angels and saints before the glory of the Lord?'

We had a reading and a prayer and sang a couple of hymns from memory and left with a different perspective from that with which we came.

Chapter Thirteen:

A Change of Pace

Alexandra roused me by pouring a container of water over my head. We have had our marital ups and downs like any couple, but this was unprecedented; not just a slosh in the face but a copious amount wetting my shirt and shorts. What had I done to deserve such a rude awakening? What was particularly odd was where I was lying: not on the airy floor of bamboo slats, but in the mud outside our Apnagan hut. As the water was poured, I thought of the waste, of the 20-minute round trip to the water pump, and the return up a steep, shadeless hillside with full containers. Another woman, gripping me under my arms, raised me into a sitting position and spoke at the same time as my wife, who was desperately trying to get my attention by speaking urgently into my other ear. Neither helped me understand what was happening. Finally the water pouring ceased.

I began to put together the pieces. We had eaten a favourite lunch, a mongo bean stew cooked in ginger, served in a bowl of rice, and then I had felt ill. Feeling the need to vomit, I had descended the hut's steps; my legs had felt weak. I collapsed and blacked out for a few seconds before being revived by all that water.

That same trip, Alexandra invited a short-term worker who was with us, to come to ring the church 'bell'. This 'bell' was the usual type, a short but broad girder of steel, hanging from a roof rafter by a coil of wire. Alexandra demonstrated with the short but weighty bar of steel how not to sound the bell, smashing a finger between bar and bell. It was a gory mess for several weeks and was yet another reminder of perhaps overdoing things.

The short-term worker did not find it easy spending nine days in Apnagan, having neither the tribal language nor Tagalog. Unable to communicate or do anything particularly useful for the Buhid frustrated her desire to serve Filipinos in some capacity. Short-term trips really were opportunities to observe and test a calling, rather than to contribute in such a setting. She found the climb up to Apnagan in 30 degrees of heat and high humidity especially demanding. Sagyom had observed how difficult the climb was for her.

'I was ready to catch her,' he told me. 'I watched her put one foot after the other, slowly moving up the hill and her legs were shaking. I thought "any moment now she will fall over" and I followed, my hands ready to catch her.' He spoke with eyebrows raised all the while, conveying amazement at how difficult she and other non-tribal people find the climb, but showing admiration too at her tenacity to go on in spite of the difficulties.

'You know,' continued Sagyom, thoughtfully stroking his neat, Lenin-like beard, 'I really appreciate the effort that she and others make to come and see us. It's good to know Christians in other parts of the world want to see us!'

I shared what Sagyom said with this girl who was bemoaning the fact she found the visit useless. From the point of view of the western work ethic, where a contribution to the general good is measured in terms of material productivity, she had indeed contributed little. But from an oriental perspective, the mere fact of being there, facing difficulties, meant a lot. The Mangyan are much maligned by their fellow Filipinos for being backward, with malicious rumours spread of their having tails, something Luktanon seriously asked us to verify on more than one occasion.

The respect and affection from foreigners raised the low self-esteem of the Mangyan. A Malaysian church twice sent a medical team. Of the seven-strong team, only one was a doctor, the remainder being professionals, giving up a week's holiday to help the medical mission treat soul as well as body.

A church in Hong Kong frequently sent many large packages of clothes which tended to fit the Mangyan better than those coming from the west and were usually of more practical use in the tropics. There were exceptions though. A young mother had pulled out of the heap of miscellaneous clothes, a long evening dress made up of brightly coloured sequins. Perhaps a wealthy Chinese lady had once worn this to casinos and other elite gatherings in the highest echelons of Hong Kong society. Sensing the garment was special and not the attire for carrying water, the Buhid mother wore this glittering costume to church on a couple of occasions, cutting an opulent and bizarre image against the squalid backdrop of earth floors and raggedly dressed farmers. She never wore it again publicly.

Leaving Apnagan after I passed out, we did not just have the usual two companions on the trail with us, but quite a gang; none of them old, nor too young, but men in their prime. A couple of months earlier, Sonja – Ernesto's wife – had contracted a high fever at the start of a music workshop she had come to teach, and had to be carried out on a home-made stretcher. Those strong Buhid had remarked to us what a weight Sonja had been to be carried over mountainous terrain for the best part of three miles and yet Sonja was a slim woman although tall by their standards. They had joked that I was not allowed to fall sick like that since they had only just managed to carry Sonja – a light weight compared to me.

I found the descent wearying and on reaching the river at the base of the mountain, I stood for a long time in the cool water as it ran pleasantly over my feet and calfs, unable to stop repeatedly yawning. The Buhid remarked on the fact to Alexandra.

Our diary was a tightly packed series of schedules made up three months in advance. We had established the practice of always arranging the dates of our next visit before leaving a village so that they felt a sense of continuity and would not feel abandoned or overlooked.

Our visits were considered a bit of a jolly by a few. Our blind neighbour at Apnagan would often greet us saying, 'How long are you with us on holiday?' Buhid do not take holidays in the sense that westerners do, but when they travel to another place for a conference or to visit relatives, this is regarded as a holiday.

But the one who was truly responsible for my deteriorating health was myself; the shadow of guilt of not doing enough, the fear of letting people down was always driving me on.

I brought forward a routine health check-up with the OMF doctor based in Manila, and had extensive blood tests, all of which revealed nothing sinister. It was strongly recommended I take things easier, a point I began to recognise, but in the meantime felt unable to do very much about, feeling duty-bound to honour the next three months' commitments in my diary. At least that was broken up by a three-week holiday with our children at Baguio up in the cool of the high mountains in the north of the Philippines.

During the holiday I started to suffer stomach pains, heartburn and vomiting after eating. Clearly I needed to pay the doctor another visit after seeing Iain and Hannah on to the plane for Malaysia.

One other responsibility had to be attended to before seeing the doctor: to locate Monay and Talad's daughter, Yomie, who had taken off to Manila a year previously and had hardly been heard of again. They suspected that Yomie was being held against her will by her employer. Tracing her proved problematic as she had moved on from her former address. Her previous employers said they did not know where she had moved. Sensing they knew more, we paused across the street to have a soft drink at a corner store and prayed, not having another lead to go on in finding Yomie. Before finishing our soft drinks, the son of the previous employer, touched by a sudden stab of conscience, came furtively over to meet us. He agreed to take us to his uncle's home down a labyrinth of alleyways we would not have found our way through, to where Yomie was now living.

We were able to converse with Yomie in Buhid which the Luktanon household was not able to understand. We ascertained that she did want to return to Mindoro, but had been prevented and kept in ignorance concerning where to go in Manila to get a homeward bound bus. We made arrangements to fetch the girl in a couple of days' time. When we did return, the employer had been most reasonable, back-paying her salary, and had even presented her with a few small gifts. We parted company at the bus station, Alexandra accompanying Yomie to Mindoro while I took a long-distance bus in the opposite direction to return to convalesce in Baguio – the outcome of my eventual visit to the doctor.

I had always envied others for wangling an enforced rest at Baguio, until I discovered the reality quite different from the expectation. I was not well enough to enjoy the location!

A retired German couple, former colleagues of ours on the tribal team, made a brief visit to the holiday home in Baguio at the same time. She was a nurse and in her Germanic manner, insisted I try her remedy for gastritis. As my medication seemed to exacerbate my condition, I was prepared to take her prescription of two to three teaspoons of yeast powder mixed in a glass of warm water. The logic of the high alkaline content of the yeast neutralising the high acidity in the stomach sounded so reasonable. Besides, she was a woman not to be argued with. I recalled how this couple, together with a number of retirees present at a conference, were asked how they had coped all those years living so publicly in the tribes. How did they handle those inevitable domestic disagreements in a home that provided no soundproofing? I will never forget her reply, 'You mean, you talk when you fight?'

They were much loved and appreciated for their genuine warmth and candid natures. The wife prodded her retiring husband to respond concerning her yeast recommendation. Had it not helped him on innumerable occasions? The quiet man put down his toast at the breakfast table and judiciously agreed, after a moment's reflection, that the remedy did indeed work. I was game to try it.

I am sure they meant well, but the warm yeast drink made me feel suddenly very unwell. With a frantic sprint from the breakfast table, leaving a half-emptied tumbler of the diabolical mixture, I found the bathroom just in time.

With my condition worsening, the doctor booked me into a private hospital covered by the health insurance OMF members had. The initial diagnosis of acute gastritis was confirmed. The hospital was really first class, but we felt guilty. Our Buhid neighbour had died from incompetence and sheer neglect, not having access to even the most basic of healthcare. It highlighted the gross inequality in a world where personal circumstances depended entirely on the good fortune (or otherwise) of which country you were born into – or which social grouping. Belonging to a despised minority group determined how others would regard you. How good heaven will be when these gross inequalities and prejudices will no longer exist.

Well once again, we soon faced another challenge of Hannah not being settled at school in Malaysia. Not being eligible either to transfer at her age to the OMF dorm at Manila's Faith Academy, we decided to home-school. Part of the success in doing home schooling depends on creating the right environment by dedicating a room (or in the limited accommodation in our town house, a corner of the living room) as a place of study. We needed a desk and a large one was available at the Calapan Mission Home – ideal except in terms of its size for transportation purposes. Before contacting a jeepney owner to make a special trip 70 miles down the coast to Bongabong, I asked one of the bus 'ductors whether it would be possible to transport the desk on the bus. We were well-known faces on this route and without hesitation, they agreed, keen to do us a good turn.

The desk, unfortunately, could not be dismantled. We stood at the wayside below the mission home with this enormous piece of furniture, with grave misgivings about getting it through the door of the bus. The bus with which we had negotiated earlier at the pier pulled up, the 'ductor seemingly unfazed by the size of the desk. Three of us heaved and shoved, turning it a degree or two this way, raising it a few millimetres more and eventually squeezed it in through the rear door. It was left upended in the corridor opposite the door, effectively barring the use of that exit and the rear two rows of seats. What were we going to be charged? The ten-plus fares of passengers who would not be able to ride in those seats? I had tried to negotiate a price beforehand but was met with evasiveness – it wasn't possible to say without seeing the desk. The other passengers did not so much as bat an eyelid with our bringing this desk on board, since folk commonly brought various articles on board that would never be allowed on buses in Britain. But no one, we reckoned, had ever brought a desk of these proportions before. However, the charge for the desk was only another couple of fares.

Home schooling meant that I spent that academic year travelling to all the village destinations on my own. We did go more than once to Batangan as a threesome; the house there was equipped with a table and chairs, making schooling more feasible. But this was still not easy since Alexandra was much in demand and therefore not that available for Hannah. The fairly constant hubbub of visitors coming to talk with us on the balcony and the crowd of young children who sometimes gathered about the door to stare at Hannah made home schooling difficult.

Hannah was removed from all the excitement she had had with her friends at Chefoo. Although she made the most of playing badminton in the street outside our Bongabong base with a Luktanon friend, it did not have the same dynamics as adventures at Chefoo. She missed climbing up to 'Primeval' – a small plateau-like feature in the thick of the jungle where the children built dens and knew the best trees to climb.

Iain found it unsettling at Faith in Manila without his sister for the very reasons we had anticipated. He perceived us in Mindoro as an item whilst he was sent away to school. This feeling increased as the situation deteriorated in a poorly functioning dorm.

Coming back to Bongabong took on a whole different meaning for me. Formerly I never relished returning there, but now it housed my wife and daughter. Bongabong gravitated more to the centre of my thoughts as I counted down the days passed up in the hills in anticipation of being together again.

Alexandra found herself suddenly without a role with the Buhid and greatly missed them although Buhid women made special trips to town to see their friend and confidant. If the Buhid were unable to visit, they would hand me notes to pass on to Xandra. These artless letters explained a tribal wife's concerns and maternal issues, asking for advice and prayer. I was a poor substitute as naturally a cautiousness existed between Buhid women and myself. Alexandra missed seeing to their health needs although there were still opportunities to accompany Buhid to the town clinic and, on Manila trips, stock up on medicines to equip me with. It was also unsettling for Alexandra, who hardly knew anyone in town, for she was encumbered by a shyness that was heightened by my not being around. Even settling into a church was problematic. The sudden appearance of the *Amerikano* was deemed either a threat to a nationalistic-minded church or promised to be the answer to all financial concerns in the churches advocating prosperity teaching.

Carrying on with some of Alexandra's responsibilities meant I had to be more mindful of pacing myself. The two months of enforced rest in Baguio provided the means of scrapping our schedule and starting all over again and on the doctor's insistence we took time off at regular intervals. Reinforced by the consequences of what would happen if I did not, I no longer felt guilty about having a break.

Every three months we had three to four nights away at a beautiful beach resort in the north of the island where no one knew us and no demands were made. There we hired a simple hut on the edge of a fine white sand beach and swam around the rocky headland to a section of coast inaccessible by land, discovering a whole chain of unvisited bays and coves. Limpid sea and a spectacular backdrop of cloud-capped peaks barely a mile from the coast made it a veritable paradise.

There we discovered the delights of snorkelling among the coral reefs, which contained a large quantity of tropical fish of such iridescent brilliance that one was left quite incredulous. Hannah came across a sea horse among the winnowing weed that obligingly wrapped its tail around her proffered finger. All this delighted us, bringing much sought-after refreshment. We could not understand why we hadn't made this a habit much earlier on, appreciating our location and recharging to face again the rigours of our tribal lifestyle. Furthermore these breaks were spiritually renewing, giving vitality to the ministry. In situations where most individuals are highly motivated and committed to the task, team leaders really need to lead by example by taking adequate rest, giving the right to those under them to similarly follow suit.

Favouring quiet beaches did have its drawbacks too. Once approaching what I had mistaken for a small pile of rocks, Hannah nonchalantly announced, 'Daddy, snake!' Just a further two paces away, right by the water's edge, was a ten-foot python lying there in a rather careless posture looking as though overcome by sunstroke.

I picked up a stone.

'What do you think you are doing!' snapped my wife. We had moved on a few paces and were at a distance I considered safe enough from the snake. But that tone made me abandon my plan of tossing a stone at the python to check whether it was still alive.

Chapter Fourteen:

Various Identities

A movement in the bushes caught my eye whilst I was bathing in the Siyangi River. Not letting on that I had noticed someone, I continued to wash myself, surreptitiously keeping the person in the corner of my eye. I was naturally wary, especially in a place like Siyangi that had far greater rebel activity than other places.

A middle-aged Bangon man was concealing himself rather poorly behind a bush, probably having spotted this white person in the river whilst on his way to his home high up in the hills. Like many from the interior who had not seen a white person before, my skin colour would suggest I was a being of the night, hence the untanned body, and therefore not a person at all. Usually when Bangon saw me, they quickened their pace, shooting nervous, furtive glances until a safe distance away, when they would stare incredulously whilst still briskly walking off. But this fellow was bold, curiosity having got the better of him, and he intently watched me launder my clothing. I could imagine him thinking, 'What sort of spirit is this?' He knew the spirit of the water, a naked white woman who would appear – watching her would bring a curse. But I was bearded with red hair and hair covered my body like that of an *aswang*, but I was all man and no part bird. What could I be?

Maybe he had heard I was really a man, one from far overseas where the sun did not shine so strongly, where the nights were long for part of the year, where water became hard enough to walk upon. He could well have heard of this foreigner coming to Siyangi to teach the words of the Creator of the heavens and the earth, and wanted to learn what sort of man I was.

One day I could not fail but notice a strongly built Luktanon some hundred metres off, standing alone for an hour just staring at me without ever changing posture. He never once broke the monotony of scrutinising my every movement by even lighting up a cigarette. I think he was making the statement that I was under suspicion and therefore was being watched. Several Buhid made a point of informing me later about that man.

Rumour began circulating outside the Buhid camp that I was gold prospecting, hence my lengthy time spent down at the river every day at mid-afternoon. This could have accounted for the Luktanon, particularly, scrutinising my every move. Mindoro is an abbreviated form of Mina d'Oro, Spanish for 'Mine of Gold'. Just at the close of the old millennium, international prospectors showed renewed interest in extracting minerals from central Mindoro and rumour abounded about a major effort to locate gold. With the increase of personnel in the area from the Department of Natural Resources, combined with my spending a couple of hours daily at the river, it was not difficult to imagine how the Luktanon began to suspect I was prospecting for gold!

The NPA were opposed to any mining activity, declaring that the mining company and government would exploit the people, spoil their land with opencast mining pits and scatter all the debris over the arable land, ruining it for future use. They also warned that many would die in land collapses and their hard toil would return a pittance of a wage. The rich would get richer whilst the poor would be exploited, corrupted and

ruined. With increased government activity in the rebels'
domain, the NPA feared their security would be
compromised. The wealth the government would
extract, would fund an infrastructure to extend and
secure the tenure of their rule into the interior, financially
justifying increased military deployment to safeguard
mining interests.

This suspicion limited my movements. Concerned for
my safety, the Buhid banned me from leaving sight of the
village. Monay wrote from Batangan instructing them
never to let me leave their sight; that I should have
someone with me at all times. I recall the group of Siyangi
believers listening to this letter being read out. One
cheekily remarked between his giggles that they could
hardly stand by me whilst I went to the toilet in the forest!
I was relieved to be given a certain freedom, permitted to
be left alone down by the river where the work of prayer
was accomplished, without which the teaching of God's
Word there in Siyangi would not have had a great impact.
I made it clear that no one was to risk their lives to save
me, for I was aware of the risk and had counted the cost.
Any resistance on their part was pointless for *fotols* were
no match for guns.

The Buhid traditionally fought their opponents
through the occult. Now with many being Christian, we
told them that their correct response would be to
intercede through prayer. We did not want the Buhid to
feel obliged to rise to a bravery that was not natural
among them, making it understood that their protection
was to be in protest only to our would-be captors. If they
failed to secure us, they were to send a runner to Ernesto
to notify him of our whereabouts and try to negotiate
our release through the Buhid network of contacts.

The NPA had recently told the Buhid that my
presence was tolerated in Siyangi and I was free to go to

Sigaw, well upriver! But for the time being, my venturing upriver was again banned. Naturally frustrated, I longed to go the four or five hours' walk from Siyangi up the Aliyanon River, over the central mountain divide, where a growing interest was being shown in the evangelistic trips made by Siyangi Christians.

The Buhid went to great lengths to establish our true identity with the NPA. In the first place, Alexandra and I were not American, but from an obscure country called Scotland, under a Socialist government, a land divided from America by a great ocean taking some two to three weeks to cross if one were to go by ship. They added we were poor, not owning any land and so 'had' to be provided for with gifts of sweet potatoes and bananas! They explained our purpose was to teach God's Word and that we made humanitarian contributions to their community through a literacy programme, healthcare development and a handicraft livelihood project. All this made the NPA tolerate our presence. The Buhid also added that our mission organisation had a policy not to pay ransom money to kidnappers!

Just as our presence in the hills aroused the suspicion of the NPA, it raised questions from Luktanon who marvelled at our freely coming and going through rebel-held territories, areas where most were too afraid to venture. Several suspected we were sympathisers and some thought us accomplices, suspicious of the several boxes (containing books and medicines) that accompanied all our trips. They were no doubt thought to contain articles useful to the rebel cause. Being a Bible teacher was just a cover in their eyes – we might even be training commandos in guerrilla warfare. Did I not look more the revolutionary with my red beard? Their stereotyped image of the missionary was of a wealthy, overweight, clean-shaven American with a private jeep, who lived in spacious, air-conditioned accommodation. Missionaries, the Luktanon figured, brought money to build beautiful church buildings, and to partly fulfil the office of social security benefactor to the poor in the community – who, in a show of allegiance, would join the missionary's church.

When I mislaid my visa papers I had to report their loss to the police in Bongabong. I tried hard to find some way around this, but the Immigration Department insisted that this was the only procedure. It is perhaps hard to understand my reluctance to approach the police. But I truly feared the inevitable assumptions made concerning our movement in the hills, of being linked with the NPA. We prayed much before I ventured down to the police station. My only previous contact with the station had been when I was stopped by a guard outside whilst innocently walking by. The guard had rudely demanded to see my papers and aggressively questioned my reasons for being in Bongabong. After that incident, I avoided walking past the police station, forced to take a circuitous route to the post office next door, which we visited every day when in town.

I entered the police station with its semi-circular array of sandbags positioned before the entrance and explained my reason for coming to an officious junior clerk who rigidly eyed me with all the superiority of his position. Having weighed the matter with a judicious air and a long silence, he informed his superior about my lost visa papers. The superior then explained the matter to *his* superior. My passport was demanded. I explained this was held in our mission's office in Manila since it was frequently required for presentation at the Immigration offices there, but presented instead a photocopy of the same. They were clearly unimpressed, evident from the disdainful way they looked at and held the paper. The most senior officer disappeared with the photocopy. A few minutes later he reappeared with a large, barrel-bellied captain, who approached with a smile.

'Come, sit down here,' the large captain said, gesturing me towards one of the hard chairs in the corridor. I sat down. 'So you speak Tagalog, that's very good! Turn your chair around, relax so you can watch TV!' A cable television screening a Filipino gangster movie held the attention of several officers and civilians milling around in the corridor.

'Why do you speak Tagalog?'

'So that I can enjoy better relationships with Filipinos,' I replied, saying precisely the phrase I had learned very early on in language school, and had been drilled to repeat over and over again until it was perfect. The phrase used to impress those who, on learning there was a Tagalog-speaking *Amerikano* in their company, would stroll over and ask this as their opening gambit. The problem back in those early days was the impossibility of sustaining the impression of really knowing their language. Within 20 seconds, disillusionment would descend over their formerly delighted features as it dawned this was only one of about ten phrases we had learned parrot-fashion. If one hoped to impress a Filipino beyond the 20 seconds, it was incumbent upon the Filipino to ask the right questions, using the precise phrasing the Tagalog course book used, otherwise we were doomed to say, 'Please repeat it again more slowly' or 'I don't understand'.

My word-perfect, beautifully pronounced reply clearly enthralled the police captain. This time the delight did not fade although this start with the grammatically precise Tagalog could not be sustained at quite the same level. A lot of pleasantries followed before being asked, what was I going to drink?

The coffee boy went off with the orders. The officer who had brought my query to the captain's attention had all this time been scrutinising the passport photocopy. He suddenly announced warmly, 'Ah! So you are British!' whereupon he lent forward with a conspiratorial air before pronouncing in subdued tones, 'Ah, James Bond!'

The captain gave him a searching look.

'James Bond is British, isn't he?' the officer turned appealingly to me.

I nodded hesitantly wondering where all this was going to lead.

'Double O seven, licensed to kill!' the captain proudly pronounced thickly in English.

They were certainly effusive, but I was not sure this was a happy development! Placing my identity as a non-American among the ranks of the likes of James Bond was a significant step, since Filipinos usually had the greatest problem in establishing the identity of anyone who looked *Amerikano* but said they were not! But the connection made with the highly professional undercover world of a secret agent, with his fascinating array of gadgets and the unscrupulous intent to win at any cost, was not altogether a happy association for a missionary who worked behind the enemy lines of the NPA!

I need not have worried, though, for the captain and his officer were so taken up by the Bond connection. It had made their day that one of Bond's own countrymen had suddenly dropped in out of the blue! They quite forgot to ask what I did and where I went, questions I am sure they would have routinely asked, given no distraction. My answers would inevitably have led to the NPA issue and the possible demands to assess how much I knew.

'So how can we help you?' the captain finally asked, after lengthy reflection of the various Bond films they knew.

The required police declaration was typed out, another drink was brought, this time accompanied by a hamburger. The police captain switched through the cable television channels, possibly in a vain search for a Bond film, much to the silent chagrin of all those engrossed in the Filipino movie, just when it was reaching its climax. No one dared to complain and many an eye now turned upon me, trying to fathom out who this was, who had so gained the captain's favour.

'If you have any problem, anyone gives you cause for concern, you just come and tell me and I guarantee that I will sort it out for you,' the captain said as he handed over the police declaration reporting the loss of my visa papers. The document stated in emphatic terms that I, having executed an exhaustive search of my home, had been unsuccessful in finding the said visa, 'which is deemed to have gone missing on a bus'! I did not argue with their interpretation of events, although I wondered how they concluded the visa papers had gone astray on a bus.

Home schooling was going well and Hannah had adopted a positive attitude even though she missed all the social dynamics of a classroom and a dorm. Our fellow missionaries, sensitive to this need, would invite Hannah to the beach, or to their homes, to cook or cross-stitch together. This reflected the Fellowship's aim to be an extended family for one another since each had left parents and siblings, nephews and nieces. These relationships were very meaningful and none more so than the friendship that Hannah enjoyed with a young and newly arrived Japanese girl – Kiho. Not only did Kiho have to come to terms with the simplicity of life in the Philippines (as opposed to high-tech Japan), but had to accustom herself to being virtually the only Asian on a predominantly European team. Kiho was formal and polite with all the senior missionaries, but with the eleven-year-old Hannah, Kiho could be more herself. They appreciated their times together enormously.

For Iain though, matters were so difficult in the dorm that he threatened to run away back to Buhid land, until the dangers of doing so were outlined. One colleague who regularly oversaw the dorm made a deal with Iain. If the occasion arose when Iain needed to run away, Angus would join him since he had never been to our tribal area! Iain seriously questioned the need for all this education when many of his Buhid peers were already farming a portion of their father's land. Iain's heart was with us and with the Buhid, a more familiar lifestyle and more agreeable than anything he could conceive of back in Britain. So what was the point in education and separation when all he wanted was a water buffalo, a piece of land and to learn from the Buhid? Although part of him was rebelling, the other part was faithful to the expectations made of him.

That Easter, Alexandra took Iain and Hannah to a progressive church that met in the conference suite of a five-star hotel. The room was, of course, air-conditioned and the thick pile carpet felt unusual to one used to concrete and linoleum at best. Before the worship leader took to what they described as a stage, the PowerPoint system projected the message that all mobiles and pagers were to be deactivated before the commencement of worship. The experience was indeed a culture shock for Alexandra, helping to lessen the shock of returning to Britain. The contrasts between Buhid land and Manila were far greater than the differences between Manila and Britain.

I recall one morning having breakfast with a number of Mangyan, eating with our hands off one large banana leaf which was laid on the ground, providing a communal plate for our rice. Finishing this, we made a two-hour hike through the hills, fording swollen rivers which reached to my armpits, traipsing along a seemingly endless trail through coconut groves to board a jeepney that bumped along a hot and dusty road, finally depositing us at Calapan pier. There we boarded a high-speed catamaran across the straits to Batangas port, then we took an air-conditioned bus to Manila.

Disembarking at a modern shopping mall, we were confronted by all the sophistication of the capital with its smartly dressed girls, who addressed one as 'sir', speaking English and flirting shamelessly with their eyes. All conceivable manner of merchandise bombarded the senses and the extraordinary array of choices of food confounded one fresh from the provinces. From simplicity to sophistication all within the space of about eleven hours!

The same day Alexandra and the children were worshipping in the plush hotel, I had climbed with a crowd of Batangan Buhid, in the dark before dawn, to a hilltop to celebrate the breaking of Easter morning. Bleary-eyed at five in the morning, I had a vivid impression of one of the elder's daughters, brandishing a flaming firebrand. The flame partially illuminated her face, revealing an animation aroused by the sense of celebrating the risen Lord. She leapt the stream with an easy fluid motion and, with her friends and family, set off with such a mad, mad pace up the hill that left my head reeling, my chest pounding to the point that I thought I was going to be sick. Her rapturous expression, lit by a sudden candescence from a flaming torch, was captured in split-second imagery, full of wonder. It exuded the glee of an anticipation that could not wait as she leapt over the broad stream and into the mystery of the darkness of the jungle on the other side. We assembled on a ploughed summit in the half-light before dawn, the eastern sky a dark blue in contrast to the black elsewhere. A fire burned on a neighbouring hill, lit by the Catholics celebrating in similar manner. Monay led us in worship, during the course of which he said, '*Faduwasay* – you will be doing the message after a couple more hymns!'

How foolish to come unprepared! I had just arrived in Batangan the night before with a strong urge to celebrate Easter in this manner. I had not even recuperated at Bongabong but had travelled from one tribal village to another, with the attitude of coming as a bystander rather than a leader. Why I had imagined that this was possible I do not know. From early on, I was taught to always be prepared, to anticipate that I could well be the one asked to preach, so I would never be taken by surprise. I did not want to tell the church I was not prepared. The Lord is gracious, for in the space of two hymns, I had put together a three-point sermon appropriate to Easter that struck home – as I noted from the expression on people's faces. With everyone seated on the summit, I descended the hill a few paces to get the gathering in my view. With the soil being loose and the slope exceptionally steep, I gradually receded further from the congregation and needed to speak up louder as I did so. In the end, I slipped off my flip-flops and anchored my toes into the freshly turned soil.

I pondered why it usually took me upwards of three hours to write a sermon once having decided on a text, when this sermon had been prepared in only five minutes. I received a favourable response; if anything, warmer than usual. My wife's reflection upon the matter was different. She told me not to be so dismayed by being enabled to put a sermon together at such short notice. After all, was it not based on the best known part of the Bible, and had I not been trained at Bible college, and had I not preached hundreds of times before? There is nothing quite like the sober observation of a candid wife to take the incredulity out of one's efforts given over to the Lord, an undertaking I had considered nothing short of the miraculous!

Back together again for the Easter holidays, Iain opted for a week in Batangan rather than time on the beach. Shortly after arriving, he came down with flu. Iain's body erupted into itchy hives as an allergic reaction to the penicillin taken. Monay came to the rescue, telling us that the sap of a banana leaf has medicinal qualities soothing to itchy skin and that they lay their children down on a freshly cut leaf when suffering from measles or chicken pox. Two leaves were cut, one laid on the floor to form a mat both longer and wider than his body, whilst parts torn from the other frond were warmed over a flame to make the sap sweat. When the leaf was moist, Monay rubbed it over Iain's affected skin, bringing quick relief.

We were called upon to mediate over a land inheritance issue. An elderly father, whose children all had homes of their own, was feeling very lonely and talked about marrying again although he had no woman in mind. This worried some of his children for the father's land was quite considerable; should he marry again, the land would become the property of the wife, if she outlived him. She in turn would probably portion it out to her own grown-up children, leaving her late husband's children without further inheritance.

Feelings were running high, especially with the youngest son who had the least land among the siblings. He was particularly anxious to secure more land, something most of his siblings supported him in. The father caught this son picking limes from his land one day (which in itself was quite acceptable even between neighbours). Owing to the growing tension, it led to an exchange of words, prompting the son to visit his father that evening demanding the land now before his father remarried. The father refused, stating that he needed land to support himself. The discussion deteriorated into a shouting match and the young son stormed out of the house. On hearing someone approaching the house shortly after, and presuming it to be the youngest son returning to do him an injury, the father armed himself with a club-like piece of wood and concealed himself behind the door frame. He brought the weapon down with considerable passion on the head of the one entering his home. It was not the youngest son but another son, who, having heard the heated argument, had come along to be a peacemaker. He was stunned and bleeding prolifically!

The church elders were involved in trying to mediate a reconciliation as too were the tribal town councillors, but to little avail. We were loath to get involved in matters far beyond our knowledge and experience. Back home this was a matter for lawyers and barristers and we felt hopelessly out of our depth. Since this entire family were all part of the church, tensions were carried into the meetings and it was clear that the matter could not just be ignored. However, since Buhid society did not have recourse to the sophistication of a judicial system beyond that of church and civic councillors, we reluctantly agreed to get involved. Our help was conditional on the church elders being present to advise about their unwritten inheritance laws. We were heavily reliant upon their wisdom and sense of fair play. These tribal lore matters differed from Philippine laws, illustrating how much a law unto themselves the Buhid were.

It transpired that the father had placed a curse on his land should the youngest son farm it. Should that son gain the right to farm his father's land upon the latter's death, the land would not yield for him and he would be afflicted with a terminal illness. The father had walked with the Lord for the major part of his life, had served as church elder on numerous occasions, but in this time of mounting tension, he had resorted to violence and to the occult. Evil had not been idle in disrupting the life and witness of the church.

The discussions were long, involving talking with the disputants separately on several occasions. Eventually we gathered the entire family, and the church elders all sat on stones or pieces of wood or squatted in shady areas outside the front door of the father's house. Everyone had something to say, but when all was said and heard, a compromise was agreed, promising the inheritance of the whole land to the youngest son after the death of the father (for this was what all the other siblings finally determined was right). In return the youngest son was to respect his father's land and his person and was not to take any of the fruit of it without his father's prior permission. The father lifted the curse by a prayer and they asked forgiveness of one another – although in forgiving one another, I felt this was done more as a formality rather than a heartfelt transaction.

Chapter Fifteen:

Farewell at Fish River

Sayna, the main elder at Safang Uyang, met me at the trading post of Nara. Strongly built and with an impetuous air, Sayna's thick hair, sweeping over his head, appeared restless. His lips were stained bright red with the chewing of betel nut, which he seemed hardly ever to be without.

He wore a heavy-looking gold watch, his pride and joy from a few years ago. Around the time of his acquiring it secondhand, Sayna had asked if I could get the right date to appear on the watch's face. Being a westerner, I was often asked to perform small favours of this kind since such technology had originated from the west. This view was verified by the impressive practical skills of previous missionaries, who, unlike myself, persuaded the Mangyan that all westerners were very skilled at fixing such things. (Or maybe it was the large number of Swiss missionaries we had on our team; their country was even known among the Mangyan for making watches.) I should have known better than to pretend that I knew what I was doing. Although I did succeed in getting the right date and day to appear in the small window of the watch's face it was at the expense of the hour and minute hands continuing to go round! I didn't know what I had done, but no amount of fiddling got it to work and I deeply regretted ever having tampered with it in the first place. In all likelihood, I was jeopardising a relationship with someone to whom I had only just been introduced. Out of sheer desperation (and rising embarrassment), I prayed over the watch and had a final fiddle with it. It worked again, which not only caused me much relief, but impressed Sayna. He held me in high regard, far beyond that of a watch repairer, after that.

We set off, just the two of us, on the lengthy trail to his village. Sayna placed two heavy boxes of Bibles and other literature that the church had requested, at either end of a carrying pole which he bore balanced upon his shoulder. The weight of all this was so considerable that he regularly pivoted the pole across the back of his neck to transfer the load to the other shoulder. Our trail passed through Apnagan where we stopped by prior arrangement for a substantial lunch, cooked by one of Sayna's relatives. Whilst the food was being cooked I was told to rest, which I duly did, falling asleep in no time after the exertion of our swift climb in the tropical heat of late morning. I suspect that the Apnagan people had impressed upon Sayna the need to look after me.

Embarrassed to wake me, they patiently waited until I woke of my own accord. At that very moment, Sayna, who had been crouching close by, evidently observing me, announced that it was lunchtime. He rose impetuously as though there was no further time to wait! The poor man was probably ravenously hungry since Buhid often forego breakfast in favour of an early start on the trail.

After lunch we proceeded along a trail little known to me; a rather disheartening trail that would rise and fall a good number of feet along the precipitous side of a ridge. Instead of the trail meandering along the contour, the Buhid had preferred a more direct line which meant plunging down into every defile and up every rising spur, taking the course that a bird would fly rather than a man, keen to conserve energy, would take. Energy was a commodity of which they seemed to have a great supply. There was no alternative route through the thick jungle other than to go along this arduous, undulating trail in the full heat of the afternoon. The view of wooded Mount Sumagui, rising bold and magnificent into the clear blue sky across the deep valley, dominated the entire route; although this was a very fine prospect and distraction, it offered no consolation of really showing any substantial progress made along the trail. Whilst I drank thirstily of the streams along the route, replacing the great quantities of fluid lost, Sayna took a few sips, spitting out half of what he took. I wondered how much further his village was. Sayna tried unsuccessfully to persuade me to give up my backpack as well, since I was now slowing down, but I was anxious to retain some dignity by carrying my own load, especially since his load was extremely heavy.

We eventually came up a steep rise where the trees thinned and, finally reaching the brow, we looked out upon Safang Uyang – 'Fish River'. This ten-house hamlet was scattered along a slight valley running at right angles to the direction of the ridge. Sayna's house was the furthest away, a few strides down from his father's house and built almost attached to the small chapel. Beyond them, the top of the hillside had been levelled off to make a basketball court, an unexpected sight so far into the mountains, but indicative of the passion that even the tribal men have for the game.

Apparently when one of the pioneer missionaries from North America had introduced one tribal group to the game, the concept of competition was very alien. It had been very hard to make them oppose a fellow on the other team by obstructing him from throwing the ball through the hoop. The Mangyan thought, why should he do such an uncivil thing to one of his fellow men? For quite a while the ball was courteously passed from one to another, regardless of what team they were in, to allow everyone the chance to try out their skill. If missionaries are accused of changing the native culture for the worse, then I would concede that here was such an example. However, basketball was already making inroads into other tribal places through Tagalog loggers who introduced the game. Furthermore, Mangyan planting rice down in the lowlands had watched this activity going on and, eventually succumbing to the lure, had also introduced the sport to their tribal villages.

'How is the watch doing?' I tentatively inquired as we rested, newly arrived at his home at Safang Uyang. I had noticed how carefully he wiped the perspiration from the watch face with a cloth.

'Fine,' Sayna replied with a smile, amused by the recollection of my fretful efforts to make his watch work again. It was probably in part due to recollecting the prayer which had fixed the watch that Sayna went on to venture, 'I was wondering whether you could pray for my wife? You see, she has been sick for a long while now; headaches, feeling weak and faint. You don't need to do it now,' he added hastily, shifting uneasily about on the floor, 'rest first, drink and eat.'

He smiled good-naturedly, revealing healthy teeth but so stained with betel nut that it looked as if he had just been chewing on raw meat. Eba, his wife, made her appearance and spoke of how her sister (who lived in Apnagan), had been restored to full health after a lengthy infirmity, following our praying for her.

Sayna took me to his storehouse across the way from his home, where he kept wood and various agricultural tools. He apologised for the very basic quarters and told me not to worry about having to cook, for Eba would include me

in the preparation for every meal. The storeroom was my
home for nine nights. The roof was quite weatherproof but
so low that I had to scramble across the floor on my
haunches (rather like Lukmoy of Apnagan, who walked
on withered legs disfigured through polio). The store had
no window but light came in through the bamboo slats of
the floor and, by sliding the door screen to one side, the
place was airy and light. My sitting by the door invited
many neighbours to come and introduce themselves. They
brought gifts, a pineapple, some star apples or avocado,
or sometimes a basket of ready cooked sweet potato which
provided a good snack. However, I was so well fed by Eba,
that most of these gifts provided hospitality for the next
visitor or for the children who always had an appetite for
more. Eba, like the majority of Hanunoo women, knew
how to cook well, stewing vegetables in the juice extract of
water-soaked grated coconut, and flavouring other dishes
with the garlic and ginger that grew prolifically in
Mindoro's hills. Hanunoo also dried several varieties of
pulses, providing nourishing dishes during the lean times
between seasons, so for once, I put on weight during this
visit rather than lost the customary two to three kilos.

I was well looked after, not even having to collect
water, for Sayna and Eba had seven helpful children.
One of their daughters showed me the way to where I
could wash. This eleven-year-old girl brought her small
brother along too and led me up the hill past her
grandfather's house at quite a pace. 'It's not far!' she
ominously told me.

The path went over the brow of the hill and down a
very steep slope to a levelled area which provided a
paddy field with a small, muddy brook that flowed
through the middle of it. Negotiating the slope in dry
season would not have been difficult and although this
was supposed to be dry season, it was uncommonly wet

A winsome grin
Dr Douglas Kennedy

and the mud was knee deep. The depth of the mud was not a problem for at least one's foot found a purchase in the somewhat resistant mass of clay. The challenge was the usual one that where the clay was so hard-packed on steep places, and offered neither convenient stone nor a few blades of grass to secure a foothold, one risked falling in the mud. I gingerly followed these two youngsters who made it look reasonably easy. They stopped and looked back at me as I descended the slope doing a kind of wild dance with my out-of-control legs and arms flailing madly in an attempt to stay upright! They giggled over the incompetent antics of this western adult before politely hiding their amusement by placing a hand across their mouths. They went on and waited around the corner so as not to embarrass me.

The Mangyan are sensitive to another's feelings. When Iain was about six, he had watched some children shin up palm trees quite effortlessly. They thrust their bodies out with their legs whilst at the same time, grasping around the back of the trunk with their hands, they pulled in their torsos. The Mangyan boys were delighted to have Iain join them but as soon as they realised he could not imitate their tree-climbing ability, they abandoned our rather unhappy son. They left him not out of impatience over his inability, but out of deference so Iain could learn without the embarrassment of others watching.

The bathing place was nothing like the swift torrent of the Siyangi River, nor the bottomless pool at the foot of the rocky flume of Manihala, but was a trickle of a brook flowing in a shallow muddy defile. Unremarkable as the place was, at least the water was clear and with the aid of a plastic scoop, I managed to get clean only to be dirtied again by the return up the muddy slope.

The rain never stopped throughout the visit, making even visiting folk around Safang Uyang village quite an ordeal. Every house was perched on a steep slope and the ground close to the main doors was well-trodden clay, smooth and extremely slippery. The approach to our home at Apnagan was much the same and I recall remarking to Alexandra, who was making even heavier work than I of descending the steep slippery slope, 'Aren't you glad that there are at least houses to hold onto to prevent you from falling?'

'I wouldn't have to be up here on this stupid hilltop if it wasn't for these houses!' she caustically replied. At that she lunged forward and would have landed in the mud had she not seized hold of Kumhay's house. Kumhay was our very elderly, blind neighbour whose home had stood for a long time. As my wife grabbed a supporting upright, the whole house keeled over dramatically to one side, alarming the blind lady inside who, thinking it was an earthquake, was panicking to get out. Alexandra was profusely apologetic. With a yank, we succeeded in getting the house to stand upright once more from its drunken angle. Amazingly no decaying support had cracked or broken with the sudden jerk; instead, the supporting stilt posts had merely shifted in their saturated, pliable anchorage. Kumhay thought it very funny, our incompetence breaking up the tedium of her unhappy lot in latter life.

The sloppy residue, just like the slip that potters use, squelched up between one's toes, sometimes with a powerful jet that reached right up the inside of the legs of one's shorts. I never ceased to be amazed by the Buhid's ability to clean their feet and legs upon a mud-encrusted rag with just a few dextrous wipes, without using their hands, or with only half a scoop of water! I never succeeded in emulating these efforts as I apologetically entered their houses, having taken three times the amount of time in the process. I was always graciously received by hosts amused by these small struggles, who, indulgently noting the trouble, were all the more appreciative of the effort made just to be among them.

The relentless rain and mud everywhere, even inside my sleeping sheet, would have demoralised me into a state of deep depression had it not been for these delightful people who so valued my presence and the teaching of the Word of God. They were hungry for Bible teaching; this was evident from their prompt attendance at every meeting, no one missing out on a single session. Their promptness surprised me at first, until I made the link with Sayna's preoccupation over his fine watch.

Timekeeping never bothered the Mangyan. This could be considered by some as a problem, waiting for folk to arrive before getting a meeting underway. Commonly it took up to half an hour from the ringing of the bell for the assembling of enough people to warrant a start. These delays no longer bothered me, if they ever did in the first place, because I would regard that half-hour arrival period as preparation time to write up notes or finish off a picture on the chalkboard. When last minute preparation was complete, there would often be some keen enthusiast, like Sagyom in Apnagan, with whom to discuss teaching or pastoral matters. In some villages it was necessary to ring the bell another time, for the first bell (to their thinking) was not taken as a summons to drop everything and come to church, but rather to finish off cooking, eating, repairing, even resting. The second bell twenty to thirty minutes later was the real summons to come.

It was different in Safang Uyang due to Sayna frequently taking note of the time. He would announce that it was another eight minutes until the meeting was due to start. Even if we had everything ready – the pressure lamp lit, the meal finished and cleared away – and I would make as to leave, he would put his hand on my shoulder and say, 'Faduwasay – there is another two minutes to go before the meeting is due to begin!' He would not leave home until waiting out those two minutes, sometimes silently watching the second hand laboriously make a couple of revolutions of the watch face, before suddenly announcing, 'It's time to go now!' Then he would lurch out of the house as though he were in danger of being late and stride up the hill with a determination to let all the other households know that, 'It is time now' as he clanged the iron girder with great deliberation. Figures emerged within seconds from out of the murky night, as though they too had mysteriously kept this ritual of holding vigil in anticipation of the appointed time. The church was full within a minute, or two at the most, with folk clutching their brand new Bibles and Buhid hymnbooks.

I sometimes wonder whether this time fixation was for my benefit? I have witnessed this obsession only on one other occasion and it was nothing to do with Sayna for he was not there.

That event was the 'Extension School', the preliminary semester's syllabus of the Mangyan Bible School. Those teaching had all been students of a quite austere Swiss missionary, a stickler for timekeeping. If new students were slovenly enough to come late to one of the lecture periods, they were reprimanded in no uncertain terms, ensuring they would never be late again. Therefore when graduates from this Bible school later held an 'Extension School', timekeeping had been so ingrained and associated with the school as part and parcel of running a lecture programme that the Buhid did likewise. Normally they were indifferent as to when a meeting started and when it ended.

Part of the necessary equipment, besides the course notes and the materials for the students, was of course the clock. No church, other than Batangan, normally had a clock, and so one had to be acquired along with the other materials. Batangan must have felt itself a little grand owning a clock, a gold-coloured plastic one rather ceremoniously carried into church in much the same way as the Bible is reverently brought in at the start of a Presbyterian service. Daginay was always the woman who carried it in and climbed up onto one of the benches to hang it on the hook. And Daginay was always the one to bring it down again, more or less around midday, irrespective of whether the meeting was still in progress or not. To Daginay, four hours of Sunday school and worship service was quite enough (and I think she was quite right), under a tin roof getting hotter by the minute as the sun reached its zenith. Sometimes meetings went on though, with the introduction of matters of church business which needed to be discussed.

The reason for this preoccupation with time at Safang Uyang, still remains something of a mystery. It can either be attributed to the quirkiness of one man's fixation with his prized watch or to a community's deference to the visit of a westerner whose culture they wished to accommodate. The irony was, if it were for my benefit, I was inconvenienced by their promptness since I had to alter my ways to accommodate their unexpected quick response to the bell, and finalise things well in advance!

On the final day of my stay at Safang Uyang, every household contributed a cooked pot of rice and a stew to provide a banquet. This was not at all the norm when I visited a village. They were so delighted their small village was deemed worthy of a visit that they insisted on celebrating with a feast. Eight days before, we had been strangers, with the exception of Sayna, whom I had of course met before. It is hard to believe how a bond of friendship can be made in just over a week! The time had been intense, every hour accounted for with either Bible teaching, literacy classes, or with visiting from house to house. Furthermore, with a community of just ten households, I did see a lot of the same people, almost hour in and hour out. Not at all used to visitors, they went out of their way to get to know me and make the most of what they realistically regarded as my one-off visit. Our acquaintance may have only been eight days long but it was already rich with hours of interaction. People shared their deepest needs: tension between in-laws, a young married couple's disharmony as they made heavy going of adjusting to one another, a new widow's loneliness, the curse a dead man left upon a field, a young man's triumph at reading for the first time and others finding the confidence and will to continue reading, a student's struggles fitting into the high school down in the lowlands, and so on. I felt very much part of their community, warming to every individual as if they were family I had known for years.

My plate was generously filled to overflowing by Buhid friends; familiar food that once had seemed strange, eaten in an atmosphere where I felt more at home than anywhere else. For once I did not miss Alexandra and Hannah down on the coastal plain or Iain up in Manila, for these people – and it seems strange to write – were my beloved too.

Some weeks later, we gathered for the inter-church conference hosted in Apnagan, marking also our last visit to Muddy Hill before returning to Scotland. Little did we know at the time that this would be the last visit for far longer than the year we had envisaged.

All those I had recently seen at Safang Uyang were in attendance too, being the next village along the ridge. More than once, after running out of things to say, we remained in one another's company not embarrassed by being tongue-tied.

Sayna was overjoyed. Before I had left Safang Uyang he had asked me how to prepare candidates for baptism. I spent time with him going through the lesson materials at the back of the Buhid hymnal prepared to give an awareness of the meaning of baptism. Not only had he used these materials for the first time with six candidates, but he went on to lead communion for the first time on his own. I was very encouraged to see the effects of a little assistance given at just the appropriate time. That was true of each of the churches, giving me peace about leaving them for a year. Certainly they were going to manage, not without mistakes, but they had reached the stage of learning from mistakes rather than being crushed by them.

The conference meetings ran from eight in the morning till late at night. The evening sessions drew together an animated throng of bodies all squashed under the heat and glare of three pressure lanterns hoarsely howling away, suspended from the roof beams. Despite the cool of evening, the close-packed quarters made everyone run with sweat. The evening meetings were lengthy, for this was the time when folk liked to perform 'special numbers'. The young people particularly would take to the front, usually in groups of between two to six. The more dynamic would accompany their worship songs with synchronised routines of arm gestures. Although they had memorised all the words, some, overcome by nerves, either could not start or would stop midway. When they faltered, the congregation would break out into a quick burst of applause to encourage, indicating they were not on their own. At this their voices picked up again, and someone would stand up in the congregation near the front, with an impatient 'sssh' and a sweep of an arm to make their point.

These conferences were popular among the youth coming from far afield, with mixed motives. The gathering provided a good opportunity to meet with the youth from other churches – a chance to see who was available. Looking for a spouse was a very important consideration when coming from one of the small churches where all the singles might be close relatives. The Buhid do not permit cousins to marry, although occasionally a very few have flaunted the taboo, much to the indignation of the whole community. No sympathy is shown for such a couple should any mishap befall them, since this is unfortunately perceived as an act of judgement.

These 'special numbers' became a focal point to see who was who; a group of lads timidly singing together often losing their voices out of nerves, letting it be known that they were there. Likewise, a group of girls, performing sweetly with carefully combed hair fixed with colourful bows, even a little bit of make-up, coyly made the same statement that they too were there. But in all of this there was usually a certain amount of sincerity in praising the Lord. The youth were all attached to the church and to varying degrees knew the Lord or were in the process of coming to a knowledge of him.

But the married were not to be outdone by the youth. They had their turn up front often doing a solo, singing very movingly in praise of the God who meant much to them, the Almighty who had released them from their fear of the demon spirits and had led them on to becoming stalwart and exuberant in the faith.

Apnagan owned the ones who delighted in singing to the Lord, who wrote their own hymns and worked hard at perfecting their worship. They were in demand throughout the whole island to lead 'worship seminars' and formed two teams to meet these requests. When certain individuals came to the front, especially the original hymn-writers, there would be a demand for total silence from a congregation that easily numbered 300. Apnagan had a character who would jump to his feet and wildly gesticulate for order. He could get quite annoyed with the congregation if they did not pay immediate attention to what he had said, sometimes petulantly demanding silence. But it worked; this was Apnagan, used to a sense of discipline, not Batangan where there was an almost irreverent disregard for order.

On these occasions, a new hymn would sometimes be first heard. If it was a hit, it would be requested many times throughout the four-day conference and thus reach high acclaim. To receive the highest accolade, many people would write down the words to the hymn and guitarists would experiment in finding just the right melody and rhythm of chords through trial and error. The melody was not always original; sometimes the tune had been heard on the radio. A song by the Carpenters is the melody to one very popular Buhid hymn. (The other notable foreign imports were not only the hymns sung in western churches translated into Buhid but also popular folk tunes like *Waltzing Matilda* and *Frère Jacques*, providing the melody for other hymns and choruses that former missionaries have introduced. We left the Buhid Church with no hymn and were probably the first missionaries to have left no such legacy. I jokingly remarked to Alexandra that the theme tune to *The Archers*, which she listened to on cassettes sent by her mother, might furnish the melody to the next Buhid hymn!)

Considering the very high standard today of indigenous hymn-writing in a place like Apnagan, a missionary would either have to be especially gifted to add anything of quality nowadays, or be rather conceited. We grew to deeply appreciate many of the Buhid hymns, particularly ones using their own traditional melodies. No longer being able to sing these on our return to Scotland became the first thing that we missed about church. In our personal devotion times we still delight in singing Buhid hymns and long for the day when we will sing them together again with our *faduwasay*, if not on this earth, then before the throne of the One who brought us together.

'*Faduwasay!*' Sagyom caught my attention as he sidled up to me, leaning against the church wall. 'Will you pray for me and Lionayan and the rest of our family? If it is the will of God, we are ready to go back to the other side of the island to share about the love and power of our Lord with those living under the fear of darkness.'

His clear, steady eyes momentarily relaxed into a smile. By the time his hand had smoothed his short imperial beard, the smile was replaced by a searching earnestness that left a deep impression upon me. These fervent words, the vision shared, struck me as being highly momentous. Many had become passionate about God, but Sagyom in his calculating lawyer-like way, had counted the cost of leaving family and fields and livelihood, and had taken the further step of committing his ways to the Lord.

Four years later when I last visited Muddy Hill, Sagyom and his wife were ready to go. The delay was understandable, covering the time it had taken to see their children through their high schooling and for the church to agree a scheme of supporting them as their own missionaries out west. Two small banana plantations had been bought through the generosity of a Scottish friend, which the Apnagan church would tend; the proceeds from the sale of bananas would support their own enterprise.

At that last meeting, Sagyom solemnly impressed upon me the need to pray.

'Pray that we will be bold to share our faith. I am so glad that people like yourselves bothered to leave everything back in your own homes to suffer to come and free us. I want to do that for Buhid living on the other side of the central mountain divide, that they may share in the gladness that we have, to be free from terror and know God's special friendship.'

Our lives had become so deeply woven with the Buhid that we ceased in one respect to be their missionaries and had become their *faduwasay*. Siblings had the closest kindred bond in the Buhid family, stronger than parent and child, because *faduwasay* grew up together, the older taking on a parental role with the younger, helping and striving together when parents were often away in their fields. We had grown up together; they had taught us their language and how to light fires, opening up our understanding to their social culture and how to best walk barefoot on wet hard-packed clay; we in turn had given them what they most desired – a better understanding of God.

They loved our children and prayed with us as we grieved their absence; we sat with them, tending to one of their children burning with tropical fever. Strong is the bond where grief over a loved one taken from this world is shared, where outrage is felt (such as when Luktanon traders consistently cheated them of the true market value of their bananas), and where joy can also be shared (as in helping a couple be reconciled and give their marriage another chance).

Was it therefore any surprise to have such deep friendships that transcended culture, race and social background? Was it any wonder, then, to know friendships deeper than with most of our own people?

I'm certain God gave us this unexpected love for a people we had not even known existed, less than a decade before; a people for whom we had been destined a long time ago.